SCOTT FORESMAN

Art

D0123777

Robyn Montana Turner, Ph.D.
Program Author

PEARSON

Scott
Foresman

Editorial Offices: Glenview, Illinois • Parsippany, New Jersey • New York, New York

Sales Offices: Parsippany, New Jersey • Duluth, Georgia • Glenview, Illinois • Coppell, Texas • Ontario, California • Mesa, Arizona

Program Consultants

Christopher Adejumo, Ph.D.
Associate Professor
Visual Art Studies
University of Texas
Austin, Texas

Doug Blandy, Ph.D.
Professor and Director
Arts and Administration Program
Institute for Community Arts and Studies
University of Oregon
Eugene, Oregon

Rebecca Brooks, Ph.D.
Professor
Department of Art and Art History
University of Texas
Austin, Texas

Sara A. Chapman, Ed.D.
Director of Fine Arts
Alief Independent School District
Houston, Texas

James Clarke, M.Ed.
Executive Director
Texas Coalition for Quality Arts Education
Houston, Texas

Georgia Collins, Ph.D.
Professor Emeritus
College of Fine Arts
University of Kentucky
Lexington, Kentucky

Deborah Cooper, M.Ed.
Coordinating Director of Arts Education
Curriculum and Instruction
Charlotte-Mecklenburg Schools
Charlotte, North Carolina

Sandra M. Epps, Ph.D.
Multicultural Art Education Consultant
New York, New York

Mary Jo Gardere
Multi-Arts Specialist
Eladio Martinez Learning Center
Dallas, Texas

Carlos G. Gómez, M.F.A.
Professor of Fine Art
University of Texas at Brownsville
and Texas Southmost College
Brownsville, Texas

Kristina Lamour, M.F.A.
Assistant Professor
The Art Institute of Boston
at Lesley University
Boston, Massachusetts

Melinda M. Mayer, Ph.D.
Assistant Professor
School of Visual Arts
University of North Texas
Denton, Texas

Reviewers

Studio Reviewers

Judy Abbott, *Art Educator*
Allison Elementary School
Austin Independent School
District
Austin, Texas

Lin Altman, *Art Educator*
Cedar Creek Elementary
School
Eanes Independent School
District
Austin, Texas

Geral T. Butler, *Art Educator*
(Retired)
Heritage High School
Lynchburg City Schools
Lynchburg, Virginia

Dale Case, *Elementary Principal*
Fox Meadow Elementary
School
Nettleton School District
Jonesboro, Arkansas

Deborah McLouth, *Art Educator*
Zavala Elementary
Austin Independent School
District
Austin, Texas

Patricia Newman, *Art Educator*
Saint Francis Xavier School
Archdiocese of Chicago
La Grange, Illinois

Nancy Sass, *Art Educator*
Cambridge Elementary
School
Alamo Heights Independent
School District
San Antonio, Texas

Sue Spiva Telle, *Art Educator*
Woodridge Elementary
School
Alamo Heights Independent
School District
San Antonio, Texas

Cari Washburn, *Art Educator*
Great Oaks Elementary
School
Round Rock Independent
School District
Round Rock, Texas

Critic Readers

Celeste Anderson
Roosevelt Elementary School
Nampa, Idaho

Mary Jo Burkwocz
Wilson Elementary School
Janesville, Wisconsin

Mary Jane Cahalan
Mitzi Bond Elementary
School
El Paso, Texas

Cindy Collar
Cloverleaf Elementary School
Cartersville, Georgia

Yvonne Days
St. Louis Public Schools
St. Louis, Missouri

Shirley Dickey
Creative Art Magnet School
Houston, Texas

Ray Durkee
Charlotte Performing Arts
Center
Punta Gorda, Florida

Sue Flores-Minick
Bryker Woods Elementary
School
Austin, Texas

Alicia Lewis
Stevens Elementary School
Houston, Texas

Denise Jennings
Fulton County Schools
Atlanta, Georgia

James Miller
Margo Elementary School
Weslaco, Texas

Marta Olson
Seattle Public Schools
Seattle, Washington

Judy Preble
Florence Avenue School
Irvington, New Jersey

Tonya Roberson
Oleson Elementary School
Houston, Texas

Andrew Southwick
Edgewood Independent
School District
San Antonio, Texas

Nita Ulaszek
Audelia Creek Elementary
School
Dallas, Texas

Tessie Varthas
Office of Creative and
Public Art
Philadelphia, Pennsylvania

Penelope Venola
Spurgeon Intermediate
School
Santa Ana, California

Elizabeth Willett
Art Specialist
Fort Worth, Texas

Contents

Unit 1

Art All Around You 16

Faith Ringgold.
*Dancing on the
George Washington
Bridge*, 1988.

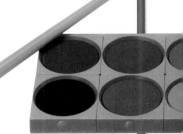

Unit 2

Look Closely at Art 50

Harry Vital. *Birds and Cattle,* 1972.

Unit 3

Forms in Art 84

Artist unknown.
Votive Statue of Eannatum, Prince of Lagash, 2600–2340 B.C.

Unit 4

Art, Then and Now 118

Katsushika Hokusai.
Woman Distracting a Child Whose Kite is Caught in a Tree, ca. 1800.

Unit 5

Artists and Expression.........152

David Hockney.
Mulholland Drive:
The Road to the
Studio, 1980.

Unit 6

A World of Art 186

Nancy Graves.
Immovable Iconography, 1990.

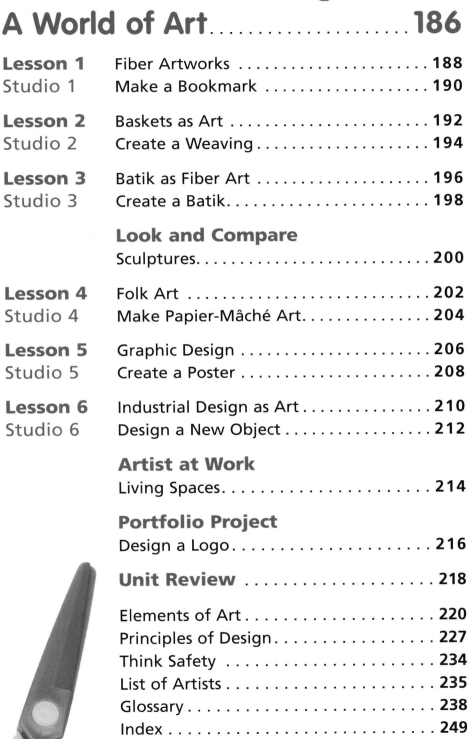

Start with Art

What is art? People have many answers to this question. Most agree that art is about expression. **Artworks** can express ideas and feelings in special ways.

Artists make artworks. Drawings, paintings, and clay pots are artworks. Quilts, photographs, and baskets are artworks too. What other artworks have you seen?

William Wegman. *Untitled*, 1991. Color Poloroid photography, 24 by 20 inches. © William Wegman. From the book *Cinderella*. Hyperion Books for Children, New York, NY.

Maria and Julian Martinez. Jar, ca. 1925. Clay with pigments, 11½ by 12 inches. Fenimore Art Museum, Cooperstown, NY.

Art is all around you. You are an artist. Name some artworks you would like to make.

How do you make artworks every day?

Your Art Words

To understand art, it is important to understand the language of art.

Your book contains many art words. They are shown in **yellow.** These words help artists talk about art.

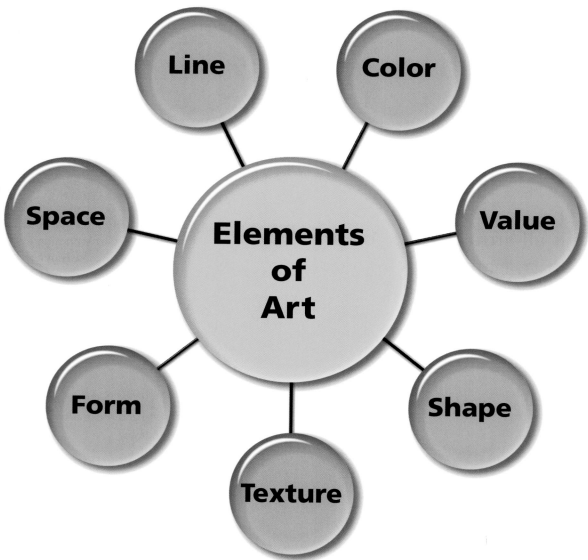

These art words name parts of an artwork.

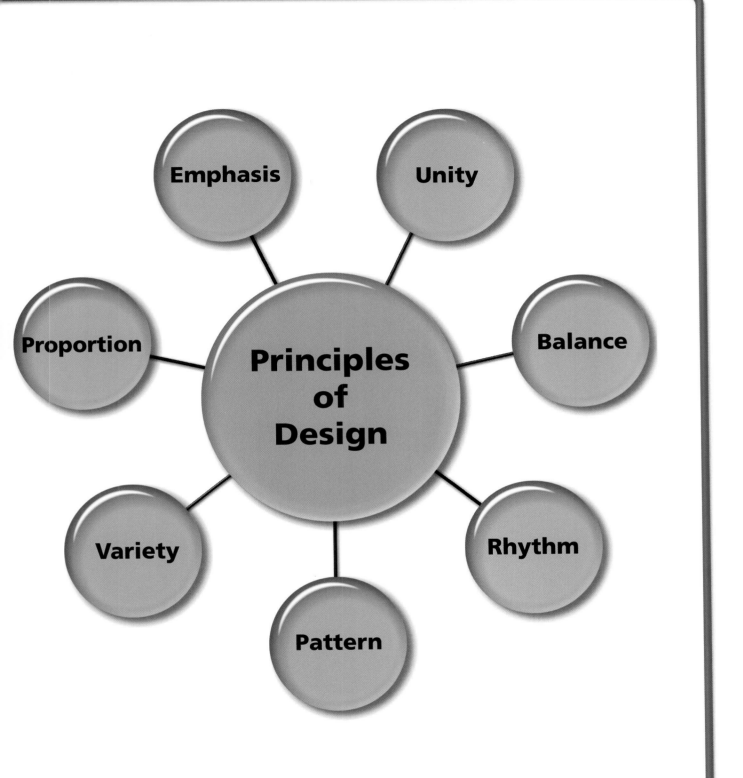

These art words tell how an artwork is put together.

Pablo Picasso. *Woman in a Red and Green Striped Beret, 1937.*
Private collection.

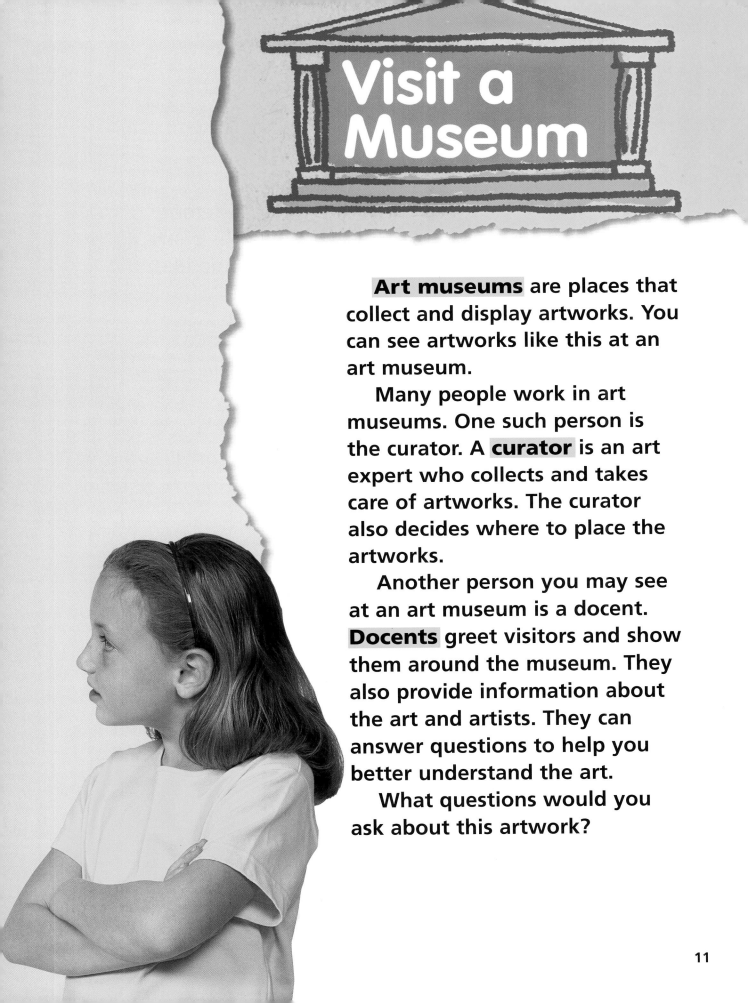

Visit a Museum

Art museums are places that collect and display artworks. You can see artworks like this at an art museum.

Many people work in art museums. One such person is the curator. A **curator** is an art expert who collects and takes care of artworks. The curator also decides where to place the artworks.

Another person you may see at an art museum is a docent. **Docents** greet visitors and show them around the museum. They also provide information about the art and artists. They can answer questions to help you better understand the art.

What questions would you ask about this artwork?

Art Tools

Artists use tools to make their artworks. Different types of tools are used to create different types of art. Think about some of the art tools you would like to explore as you make your own artwork.

Chalk pastels and artists' pencils can be used for drawing.

Artists often experiment with many types of paint-brushes and other tools when painting.

These tools are used to make beautiful mosaic designs.

Ink, paint, sponges, and a roller called a brayer, are tools used in printmaking.

When artists make clay sculptures, they use some of these tools.

Photography is the art of taking pictures. The most important tools for photography are a camera and film.

Make a Portfolio

Artists often keep their artworks in a portfolio. You can store your flat artwork in a portfolio too.

Follow these steps to make a portfolio. Use it to share your artworks with others.

1 Use two sheets of poster board. Write your name across the top of one sheet.

2 Place one sheet over the other. Be sure your name is on the front.

3 Tape the bottom and sides of your portfolio.

4 Use colored markers to decorate your portfolio.

Make a Sketchbook Journal

Many artists plan by drawing sketches. Sketches can help them remember what they have seen or imagined. Artists also record their thoughts and feelings with their sketches.

A sketchbook is a special tool. In it, artists can draw, paint, and even write their ideas. Later, they can use their sketches as a starting place for a larger artwork.

Look at these sketches by Georgia O'Keeffe. Where do you think the artist was when she made them?

Georgia O'Keeffe.
Caricatures of teachers from
The Mortar Board yearbook.
1905. Courtesy of Chatham
Hall, Chatham, VA.

Follow these steps to make a Sketchbook Journal.

1 Fold eight sheets of drawing paper in half.

2 Staple the sheets together along the fold.

3 Fold and staple a construction paper cover.

4 Decorate the cover. Write your name on it.

Faith Ringgold. *Tar Beach,* 1988. From the Women on a Bridge Series. Acrylic on canvas with pieced fabric border, 74 by 69 inches. The Solomon R. Guggenheim Museum, New York.

Art All Around You

Artists find ideas for art everywhere. They use **elements of art,** or line, color, shape, value, texture, form, and space, to turn ideas into an artwork. These elements are organized in special ways by using the **principles of design,** or unity, variety, emphasis, balance, proportion, pattern, and rhythm. What will be *your* special way of creating artworks?

Meet the Artist

Faith Ringgold is known for her story quilts. *Tar Beach* tells about growing up in Harlem, New York. What else does this story quilt tell you about Faith Ringgold?

Look for another story quilt by Ringgold later in the unit.

Line

A **line** is a continuous mark on a surface. Most lines are created by a pen, a pencil, or a brush. Find thick, thin, and wavy lines in this painting.

Vincent van Gogh. *The Café Terrace on the Place du Forum Arles, at Night,* 1888. Oil on canvas, 31⅔ by 25½ inches. Rijksmuseum Kröller-Müller, Otterlo, Netherlands.

Types of Lines

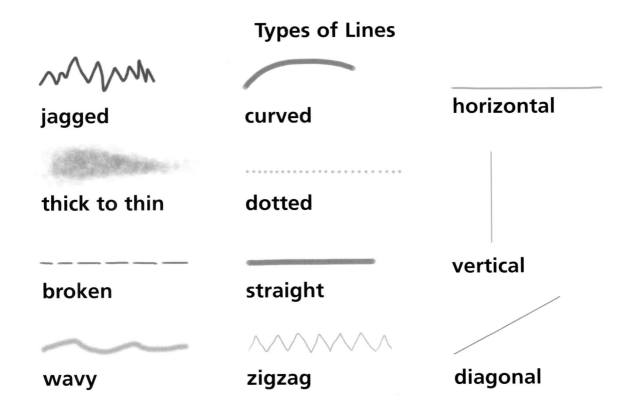

jagged

curved

horizontal

thick to thin

dotted

vertical

broken

straight

wavy

zigzag

diagonal

Horizontal lines show a peaceful scene. Vertical lines suggest strength. Diagonal lines bring motion and energy to an artwork. Find these three kinds of lines in Van Gogh's painting.

Artists use different **media** to create artworks. Van Gogh chose oil paints as his medium. Other media are pencils, paints, chalk, clay, and crayons.

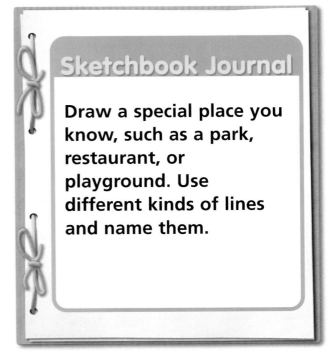

Sketchbook Journal

Draw a special place you know, such as a park, restaurant, or playground. Use different kinds of lines and name them.

Studio 1

Draw Lines

What are your favorite foods? Do you like tacos best or colorful salads? Follow these steps to draw them.

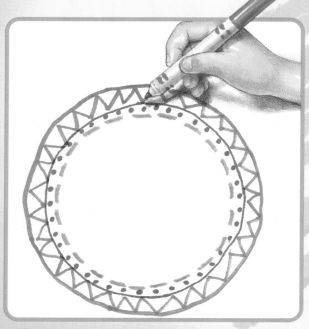

1 Draw a large plate shape. Decorate the edge with many kinds of lines.

2 Draw a glass and a drink. Add your favorite foods to the plate.

Technique Tip

Use the tip of the marker to make thin lines and dots. Use the side of the marker to make thick lines.

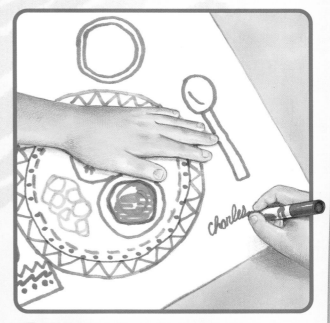

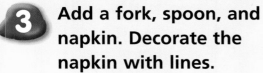 **3** Add a fork, spoon, and napkin. Decorate the napkin with lines.

4 Sign your drawing.

Think Like an Artist

Imagine that you had shown only one type of line. How would that change your drawing?

Shape

Draw a circle in the air with your finger. You have made a **shape.** Circles, squares, rectangles, and triangles are the basic **geometric shapes.** Irregular shapes you find in nature are called **organic shapes.** Find both kinds of shapes in this painting.

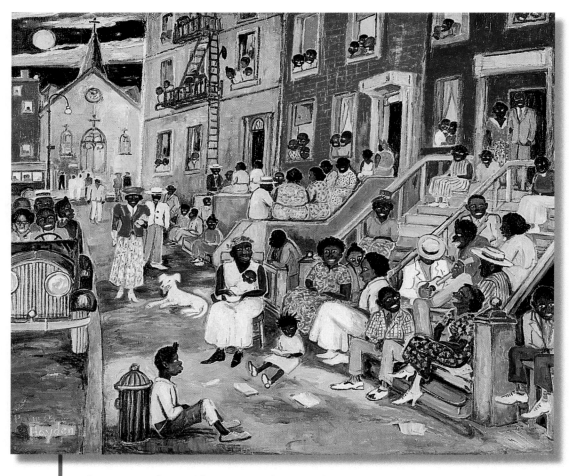

Palmer C. Hayden. *Midsummer Night in Harlem,* 1938. Oil on canvas, 25 by 30 inches. Palmer C. Hayden Collection. Gift of Miriam A. Hayden. The Museum of African American Art, Los Angeles.

Shapes

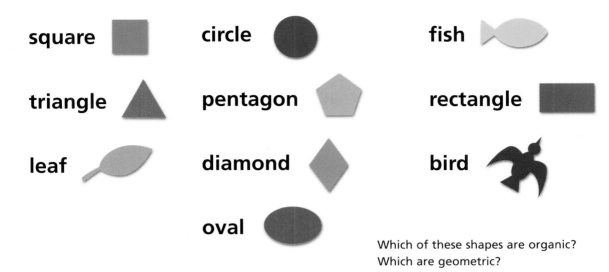

square

circle

fish

triangle

pentagon

rectangle

leaf

diamond

bird

oval

Which of these shapes are organic?
Which are geometric?

Palmer C. Hayden. *Midsummer Night in Harlem* (Detail).

A **detail** is a small part of a larger artwork. Sometimes details are enlarged. Look for organic and geometric shapes in this detail from the painting on page 22.

the painting on page 22.

Sketchbook Journal

Draw a scene of a summer night. Use both geometric and organic shapes. Write some sound words to describe what you might hear.

Studio 2

See Details

Make a detail detector to track down shapes and details all around you. Follow these steps.

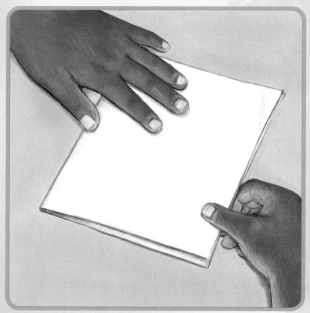

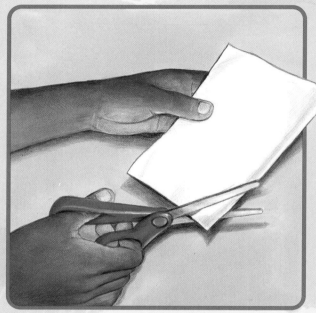

1 Fold a paper in half one way and then the other way.

2 Snip off a triangle at the corner where the folds meet.

Technique Tip

As you draw the detail, press down hard to make a dark line. Press lightly to make a light line.

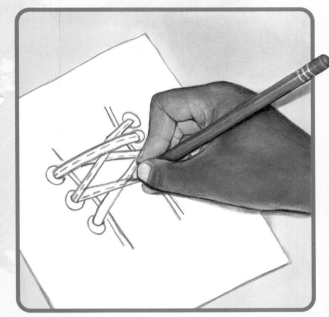

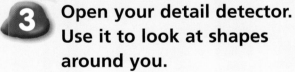 **Open your detail detector.
Use it to look at shapes
around you.**

4 **Use crayons or colored
pencils to draw some
interesting details.**

Think Like an Artist

What are some interesting features of the
details you drew? What shapes did you use
in your drawing?

Texture

The way a surface looks and feels is its **texture.**
A real cactus has a prickly texture. When an artist
paints a picture of a cactus, he or she paints sharp
thorns to show texture. Name some other textures
in this painting.

Carmen Lomas Garza. *Abuelitos Piscando Nopalitos (Grandparents Harvesting Cactus),* 1980.
Gouache painting, 11 by 14 inches. © 1980 Carmen Lomas Garza.
Collection of Richard L. Bains and Amalia Mesa-Bains, San Francisco, Calif.

Carmen Lomas Garza. *Abuelitos Piscando Nopalitos* (Detail).

This detail shows how people harvest a prickly cactus without touching it.

Some textures are only **visual textures.** You can see them, but you cannot feel them. The jacks have a shiny visual texture.

Other textures are **tactile textures.** That means you can actually feel them with your fingers. Describe the tactile texture of a kitten.

Art in My World

Look for advertisements that include photos. Describe some of the objects you see. How many different textures can you find?

27

Make a Rubbing

Work with friends to create a texture garden. Follow these steps.

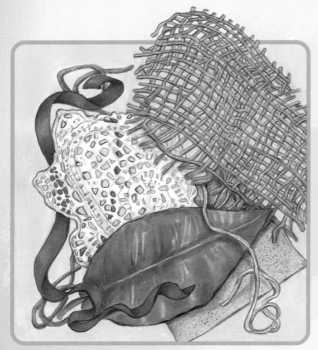

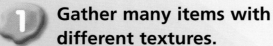 Gather many items with different textures.

2 Make a drawing of organic shapes such as flowers or leaves.

Technique Tip

Peel the paper off the crayons. Place your paper over a textured surface. Use the sides of the crayons to create a rubbing.

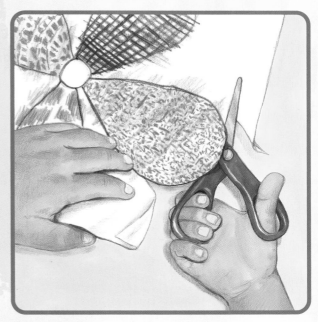

3 Put a different texture under each shape. Rub with a crayon.

4 Cut out your shapes. Make a texture garden with your friends' shapes.

Think Like an Artist

What kinds of lines created each texture in your rubbing? Point to dotted, wavy, jagged, straight, or curved lines.

Look and Compare

Bridges

Both of these artworks show bridges. But the artworks look very different. Why?

Faith Ringgold. *Dancing on the George Washington Bridge,* 1988. From the Women on the Bridge Series #5. Acrylic on canvas, 68 by 68 inches. Private collection.

Utagawa Hiroshige.
Bamboo Yards, Kyobashi Bridge, 1857. Woodblock color print, 36 by 23½ inches. Brooklyn Museum of Art, Brooklyn, NY.

Compare the lines in each artwork. What kinds of lines did the first artist use to show activity? What kinds of lines did the second artist use to show strength and peacefulness?

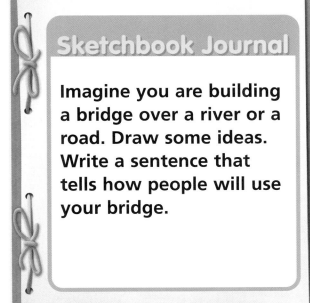

Sketchbook Journal

Imagine you are building a bridge over a river or a road. Draw some ideas. Write a sentence that tells how people will use your bridge.

Symmetry

This painting shows **balance.** It is arranged so that each part seems equally important. The flower also shows **symmetry.** Both sides are about the same. Look around you for something else that shows symmetry.

Georgia O'Keeffe. *Red Canna,* ca. 1923. Oil on canvas, mounted on masonite, 36 by 29⅞ inches. Collection of The University of Arizona Museum of Art, Tucson. Gift of Oliver James, 50.1.4.

Many things in nature show symmetry. How does a butterfly show symmetry? Describe the symmetry of a face.

This dinosaur shows **asymmetry.** The two sides do not look the same.

Sketchbook Journal

Draw two pictures. Show symmetry in one picture. Show asymmetry in the other. How would the world be different if everything showed symmetry?

Paint with Symmetry

Choose an organic shape from nature. Follow these steps to create a painting with symmetry.

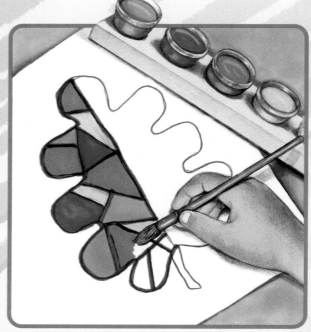

1 Draw your shape so that it fills the paper.

2 Paint lines and shapes on one side of your shape.

Technique Tip

To clean your brush between colors, dip in water and swish. Wipe the brush on the edge of the container. Then blot it on a paper towel.

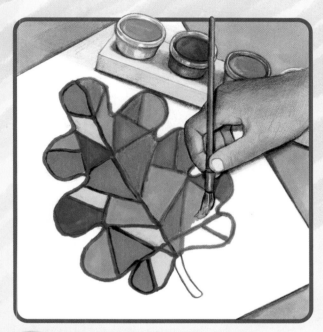

3 Use different colors to paint the same lines and shapes on the other side.

4 Share your painting with your friends.

Think Like an Artist

Which side of your symmetrical painting do you like better? Why?

Radial Balance

Point to the center of this dome. The lines and shapes spread out equally all around the center. This dome shows **radial balance.**

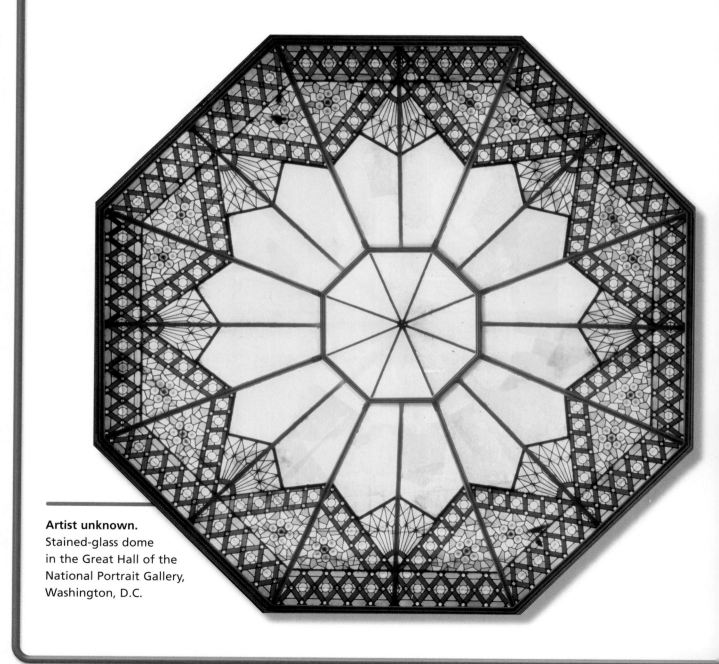

Artist unknown.
Stained-glass dome
in the Great Hall of the
National Portrait Gallery,
Washington, D.C.

How is this photograph of a sunset different from the stained glass?

The pattern in the stained glass looks like a sunset. The sunset is not **realistic**—you would never see it in real life. It is **abstract.** Abstract art often has geometric shapes and bright colors. What geometric shapes do you see in the stained glass?

Sketchbook Journal

Draw a picture showing what happens when you toss a stone into a pond or pool. Can you think of other examples of radial balance in nature? Name them.

Make a Mosaic

A mosaic is something like a puzzle. It is made by fitting together small pieces of colored objects, such as paper.

1 Choose something that shows radial balance.

2 Tear construction paper of different colors into small pieces.

Technique Tip

Begin at the center. Work outward to create your design.

3 On black paper, arrange the pieces in the radial design you chose.

4 Glue the pieces of paper close together.

Think Like an Artist

What does your mosaic say about the object you chose? Tell a friend about its meaning.

Space

The area that is in and around shapes is called **space.** Look at the first picture. **Positive space** is the shape itself. What do you see in the positive space?

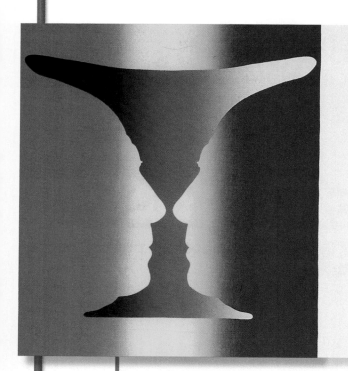

Jasper Johns. *Cups 4 Picasso,* 1972. Lithograph, printed in color, composition: 14⅛ by 32¼ inches. The Museum of Modern Art, New York. Gift of Celeste Bartos. ©1998 Jasper Johns/Licensed by VAGA, New York, NY. Photograph © 1996 The Museum of Modern Art, New York.

Usually, your eye goes to the positive space first. What is the positive space in this photograph?

Now look at the second picture on page 40. Describe its positive space.

Negative space is the empty area around a shape. How did the artist change the same spaces from positive to negative?

Research

The artworks of M. C. Escher show positive and negative space. Find one of his artworks and show a friend the positive and negative spaces.

Make a Cut-out Picture

Create an artwork that shows both positive and negative space. Follow these steps.

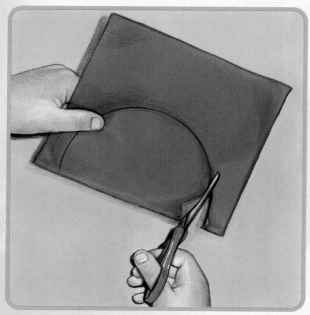

1 Cut out shapes from different colors of paper. Save the scraps!

2 Arrange all the positive and negative shapes on a sheet of white paper.

Technique Tip

To cut a shape easily, fold the paper in half. Cut half the shape from the creased side of the paper. Then unfold the paper.

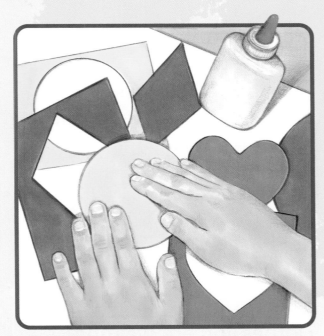

3 Glue down the shapes in your own design.

4 Color in the shapes with many kinds of lines and colors.

Think Like an Artist

Ask a friend to look at your artwork. Together, find one positive shape and one negative shape.

Story Cloths

Yang Fang Nhu is an artist with many stories to tell. She uses fabrics, or cloths, and fibers, such as thread and yarn. Look at the story cloth she made to tell about a long journey from China to Laos.

To make her artwork, Fang Nhu sewed pictures and symbols onto a large piece of cotton cloth. This story cloth shows her people, the Hmong (mung), walking to their new homeland. Follow the path they take with your finger.

Some artists, like Fang Nhu, use fabric and fibers in their work. Can you think of another career in which people work with fabric and fibers? Hint: Look at the clothes you are wearing!

Yang Fang Nhu makes story cloths.

Yang Fang Nhu. *Story Cloth,* 1978 (Hmong). Embroidered on cotton, 55 by 38 inches. Photograph by Michael Monteaux. International Folk Art Foundation Collections at the Museum of International Folk Art, Santa Fe, NM.

Create Scratch Art

Make a scratch art picture of a neighborhood scene. Before you begin, decide whether your picture will be symmetrical or asymmetrical.

1 Use crayons to cover a piece of tag board with lines and shapes. Use many colors.

2 Paint over the lines and shapes with black tempera paint.

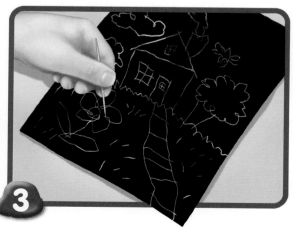

3 Use a toothpick to scratch your scene into the dried paint.

4 Use lines to show different textures.

Kalyn, Age 9. *Home Tweet Home.*
Crayon and tempera.

Brooke, Age 8. *Untitled.* Crayon
and tempera.

Look at the scratch art
these students made of their
neighborhood.

Share Your Art

1. Point to different shapes and lines you used
in your artwork.

2. Did you decide to show symmetry or
asymmetry in your picture? Explain why.

Think About Art

Read the art words. Then point to a picture that matches each word.

shape   texture   negative space
asymmetry   detail   radial balance

Write About Art

Choose an artwork from one of the lessons in Unit 1. What lines, shapes, and textures do you like in it? Write about them.

Talk About Art

• Choose an artwork from your portfolio. Maybe it was the most fun or the hardest to do.
• Tell a partner how you feel about it, and why. Use words and ideas from this unit.

Marc Chagall. *The Musician,* 1912–1913. Oil on canvas, 74 by 62¼ inches. Stedelijk Museum, Amsterdam, Netherlands.

Put It All Together

1. What lines and shapes did the artist use?

2. Is the painting balanced? Explain your answer.

3. What does the painting make you think about?

4. Do you like the way the artist expressed his ideas and feelings? Tell why.

M.C. Escher. *Rind,* 1955. Wood engraving in four colors, 13½ by 9⅛ inches.
Private collection.

Unit 2

Look Closely at Art

Artists see the world in their own special ways. M. C. Escher used his imagination to make his artwork. You can use your imagination for art, too. Look around. Where do you see designs and ideas for art?

Meet the Artist

Maurits Cornelis Escher studied architecture but instead became a graphic artist. He liked to sketch what he saw in nature. Some people consider his artworks to be like riddles. Their details look real, but the mind knows that they are impossible.

M. C. Escher. *Self-Portrait,* 1929.

Color

Artists use many kinds of colors. Notice all the **colors,** or hues, in this painting. Find red, yellow, and blue. These are the **primary colors.** *Primary* means "first" or "most important." Some other colors come from mixing two primary colors together.

Stuart Davis. *Swing Landscape,* 1938. Oil on canvas, 88 by 176 inches. Indiana University Art Museum, Bloomington. © 1998 Estate of Stuart Davis/Licensed by VAGA, New York. Photograph by Michael Cavanagh, Kevin Montague.

Color Wheel

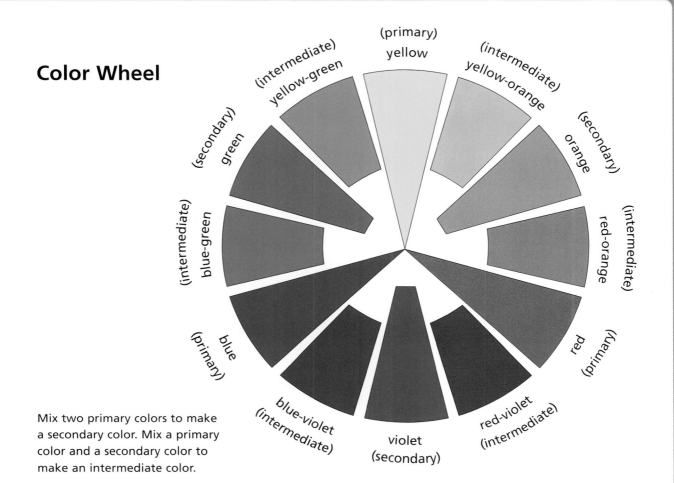

(primary)
yellow

(intermediate)
yellow-green

(intermediate)
yellow-orange

(secondary)
green

(secondary)
orange

(intermediate)
blue-green

(intermediate)
red-orange

blue
(primary)

red
(primary)

blue-violet
(intermediate)

red-violet
(intermediate)

violet
(secondary)

Mix two primary colors to make a secondary color. Mix a primary color and a secondary color to make an intermediate color.

Find orange on the color wheel. It is a **secondary color.** You can make it by mixing the two primary colors yellow and red.

Now find red-orange. It is an **intermediate color.** Make red-orange by mixing red, a primary color, with orange, a secondary color. What two colors should you mix to get blue-violet?

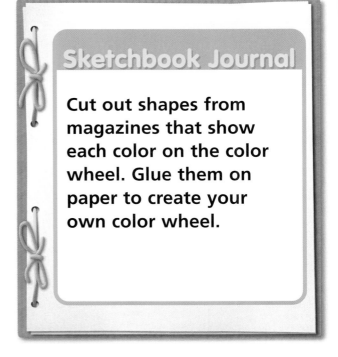

Sketchbook Journal

Cut out shapes from magazines that show each color on the color wheel. Glue them on paper to create your own color wheel.

Blend Your Own Colors

Create a painting using colors you have mixed.
Follow these steps.

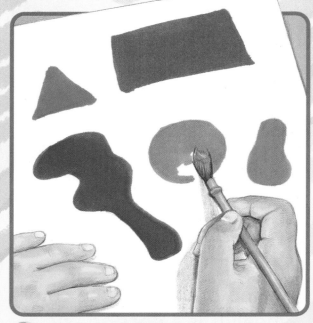

1 Mix your own secondary and intermediate colors.

2 Paint different shapes all over a large sheet of paper.

Technique Tip

To make violet, mix blue and red, then a dab of white. This keeps the violet from becoming too dark.

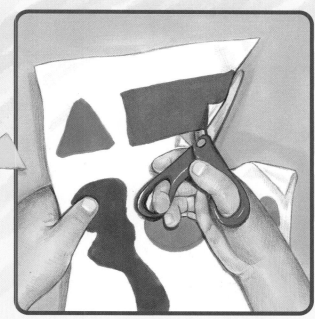

3 Cut out the shapes after they are dry.

4 Put the shapes in a pleasing arrangement. Then glue them down.

Think Like an Artist

Name the types of colors in your painting.

Color Families

The sky in this painting is filled with reds, oranges, and yellows. These colors are related. In fact, they belong to the same color family. On the color wheel on page 53, find other related colors.

Georgia O'Keeffe. *From the Plains I,* 1953. Oil on canvas, 47¹¹⁄₁₆ by 83⅝ inches. The McNay Art Museum, San Antonio, TX.

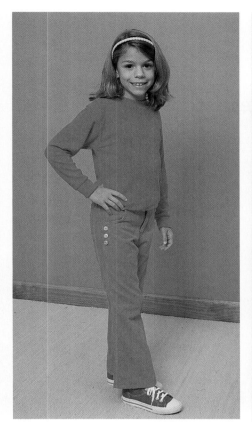

Warm colors remind people of warm feelings, warm places, and warm things. Which photograph shows warm colors?

Cool colors bring to mind cool feelings and places. Which photograph shows cool colors?

Black, white, and gray are **neutrals.** They are not on the color wheel. Which photograph shows neutrals?

Sketchbook Journal

Choose some of your favorite warm or cool colors. Use these colors to draw a picture of yourself. Do you look warm or cool?

Draw a Sunset

Use oil pastels to draw a sunset. Follow these steps.

1 Practice blending related colors from a color family.

2 On another sheet of paper, lightly draw a sunset with your oil pastel.

Technique Tip

To make strong colors, press lightly. Then rub gently with a tissue or your finger until the white paper does not show through.

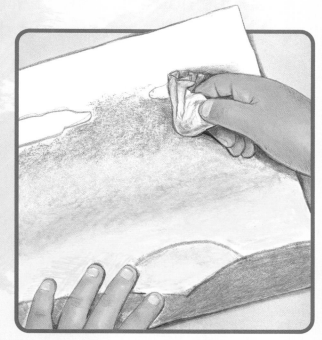

3 Color the sunset by blending related warm colors.

4 Color the ground and the upper sky by blending related cool colors.

Think Like an Artist

How did blending or rubbing the oil pastels change your sunset?

Color and Value

Artists show colors with different values. Notice that the blues in this painting are not all the same. One house is light blue. Another house is a darker blue. The lightness or darkness of a color is its **value.**

Gabriele Münter.
Schnee und Sonne (Snow and Sun), 1911. Oil on cardboard, 20 by 27½ inches. The University of Iowa Museum of Art, Iowa City. Gift of Owen and Leone Elliott. 1963.63.

tint

shade

To make a lighter blue, the artist added a dab of blue to white. A lighter value of a color is called a **tint.** Adding black to primary blue makes a darker blue. This darker value is called a **shade.** Mixing white or black with any color changes its value.

Research

Even cave artists used color. To make "paint," they mixed minerals with spit or animal fat. Find a picture of a cave painting. What colors are in it?

Studio 3

Paint a Scene

Think of a city street with buildings of different shapes and sizes. Use tints and shades to paint a picture of the scene.

1 Arrange some cartons to look like buildings in a city.

2 Mix tints and shades. Add some thinned glue.

Technique Tip

Mix your colors on plastic lids. Add a dab of color to white to mix a tint. Add a dab of black to a color to make a shade.

3 Paint the buildings. Use tints and shades to show windows and doors.

4 Use a small paintbrush to add details to your painting.

Think Like an Artist

Were you satisfied with the tints and shades you mixed? Tell why or why not.

Nature Scenes

Notice the birds in these artworks. The artists used color values to make the birds stand out or to keep them hidden.

M. C. Escher. *Sun and Moon,* 1948. Woodcut in green, red, gold and black, printed from four blocks, 9⅞ by 10⅝ inches. © 1996 Board of Trustees, National Gallery of Art, Washington, D.C., Cornelius Van S. Roosevelt Collection.

Harry Vital. *Birds and Cattle,* 1972. Oil on canvas, 28 by 56 inches. Texas Southern University, Houston, TX.

The first artwork shows lighter values filling organic shapes. The second artwork shows darker values filling mostly geometric shapes. Squint your eyes to help you see the sun and moon in Escher's woodcut. Do the same to see the birds and cattle in Vital's painting.

Sketchbook Journal

Draw some shapes that fit together. Experiment with lines and colors to make your shapes hard to find or easy to see. Put some dark shapes next to light ones to help your eye see the shapes.

Landscapes

A **landscape** shows an outdoor scene. In this landscape, the women gathering grain appear near the bottom of the painting. Objects in the **foreground** of a painting seem closest to the viewer. What do you see in the distance, or **background,** of this landscape?

Jean Millet. *The Gleaners,* 1857. Oil on canvas, 32½ by 43⅓ inches. Musée d'Orsay, Paris, France.

How does the artist use size to show objects in the foreground and background?

Point to the field in this painting. The area beyond the women is known as the **middle ground,** between the foreground and the background.

One woman looks closer than the others. Artists **overlap** objects to create a sense of space and distance. Find other objects that appear close to you.

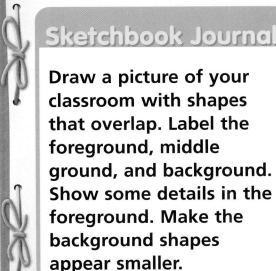

Sketchbook Journal

Draw a picture of your classroom with shapes that overlap. Label the foreground, middle ground, and background. Show some details in the foreground. Make the background shapes appear smaller.

Draw a Landscape

Think of a real or imaginary landscape. Follow these steps to draw it.

1 Begin drawing at the bottom of your paper to show shapes that are near.

2 Draw more shapes in the middle.

Technique Tip

To practice overlapping, begin by drawing foreground shapes. Add parts of some other shapes behind those.

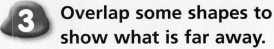

3 Overlap some shapes to show what is far away.

4 At the top, draw small shapes for what is farthest away.

Think Like an Artist

How well did you succeed in making things look near and far away in your drawing? Explain.

Center of Interest

Many paintings have a center of interest. The **center of interest** is what you notice first. What is the center of interest in this painting?

Mary Cassatt. *The Child's Bath,* 1893. Oil on canvas, 39½ by 26 inches. The Art Institute of Chicago, Chicago, IL.

Johannes Vermeer.
The Kitchen Maid, ca.1658.
Oil on canvas, 17¾ by 16
inches. Rijksmuseum,
Amsterdam, Netherlands.

What are the girl and the woman looking at in *The Child's Bath*? How did the direction of their gaze help you find the center of interest? The **emphasis** on the child and her foot creates the center of interest.

Color, size, or placement can create emphasis. In Vermeer's painting, what is the center of interest? How did Vermeer create emphasis?

Sketchbook Journal

Draw yourself doing something you do every day, such as tying your shoes or eating a meal. Use emphasis to make the center of interest stand out.

Studio 5

Draw with Emphasis

Show yourself playing a game or doing an activity. Use emphasis to create your center of interest.

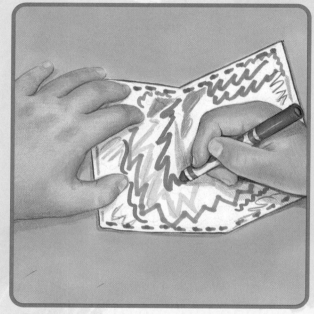

1 Cut out a shape that represents your favorite game or activity.

2 Decorate the shape to make it stand out.

Technique Tip

One way to show emphasis is with size. You can make the center of interest big. You can also show emphasis with a bold color.

3 Glue the decorated shape onto a sheet of paper.

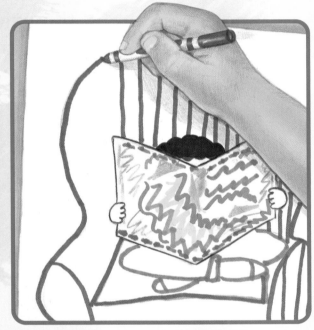

4 Add yourself doing this activity. Add other details, too.

Think Like an Artist

How did you show emphasis in your drawing?

Unity and Variety

Pat Steir showed many elements of art in this painting. She combined shapes, colors, and other elements to create **variety.** Even though each rectangle is different, the painting looks complete. This quality gives the painting **unity.**

Pat Steir. *The Brueghel Series (A Vanitas of Style)*, 1982–1984. Oil on canvas, 64 panels: each 28½ by 22½ inches. Courtesy Robert Miller Gallery, New York.

Each rectangle is painted in the style of an artist that Pat Steir admires.

William H. Johnson. *Flowers,* 1939–1940. Oil on plywood, 38½ by 25⅜ inches. Smithsonian American Art Museum, Washington, D.C.

A **still life** can be a painting, picture, or photograph. It shows objects, such as flowers or food, that cannot move on their own. William Johnson painted this still life of flowers in a vase. How did he show variety?

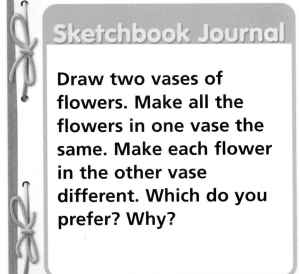

Sketchbook Journal

Draw two vases of flowers. Make all the flowers in one vase the same. Make each flower in the other vase different. Which do you prefer? Why?

75

Paint a Still Life

Work with friends to create a still-life puzzle of a bouquet of flowers. Follow these steps.

1 Look closely at a still life of flowers in a vase. Paint a picture of it. Let it dry.

2 Fold the painting twice one way. Then fold it twice the other way.

Technique Tip

Use as much of your paper as you can when you paint. That way, each piece of your puzzle will show part of the still life.

3 On the back, number the rectangles from 1 to 9. Cut them out. Trade them.

4 Put your rectangles in order. Glue them. Leave space between the pieces.

Think Like an Artist

How does the artwork you and your friends created show both unity and variety?

Living Artworks

Patricia Hammer is a topiary (TOPE ee air ee) artist. She makes shapes from different kinds of plants. These musicians are made of ivy. They cannot play a note of music, but they make people smile.

To create the musicians, Hammer began with steel frames shaped like people. She stuffed the frames with wet moss. At the same time, she planted ivy in the moss so that the moss was completely covered.

Hammer's artworks are never quite finished. That is because the plants keep growing. She has to trim them to keep the forms she wants.

Hammer thinks of topiary as a living art. Do you agree with her? Explain why.

Artist Patricia Hammer uses plants as her medium.

Pat Hammer. *Mariachis,* 2003. Moss and ivy on metal frame, 72 inches high. The Philadelphia Flower Show, Philadelphia, PA. Photography: Rachel Cobb.

Make a Painted Collage

Use pictures from magazines to make a collage on a painted background.

1 Mix tints and shades to paint a foreground, middle ground, and background.

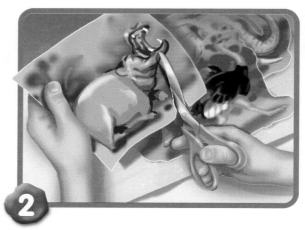

2 Find outdoor pictures in magazines. Cut out people, animals, and objects.

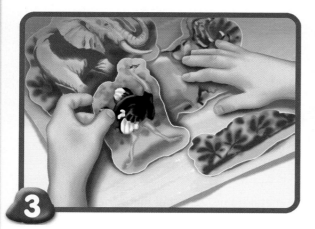

3 Choose one picture to be the center of interest. Arrange your images.

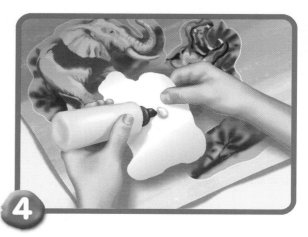

4 Decide which way looks best and glue the pictures down.

Sidney, Age 8. *In the Wild.* Collage.

Riley, Age 8. *Jet.* Collage.

What is the center of interest in these collages? How did the artists show emphasis?

Share Your Art

1. Point to images in the foreground, middle ground, and background of your collage.

2. Tell how you used emphasis to create the center of interest.

Unit Review

Think About Art

Read the art words. Then point to a picture that matches a word. A picture can match more than one word.

variety	cool colors	center of interest
still life	overlap	neutrals

Write About Art

Find a scene you would like to paint. What would be the painting's center of interest? Write about how you would use emphasis.

Talk About Art

- Look through your portfolio.
- Choose your favorite artwork.
- Describe the artwork to a friend. Use words from this unit, such as *primary colors, foreground, emphasis, variety,* and *tint.*

Janet Fish. *Fallen Vase,* 1987. Oil on canvas, 70 by 48 inches. Robert Miller Gallery, New York, NY. © Janet Fish/Licensed by VAGA, New York, NY.

Put It All Together

1. Where do you see warm and cool colors?

2. What part of the painting do you notice first?

3. What do you think the artist was saying about nature?

4. Do you like the way the artist expressed her ideas or feelings? Explain your answer.

Henry Moore. *King and Queen,* 1952–1953. Bronze, 66⅓ by 58 by 37 inches. Tate Gallery, London.

Forms in Art

Artists express themselves in different ways. Some draw. Others paint, carve, or join materials into **forms** you can go around. You can look at forms from more than one side.

A form takes up space. Some forms are **sculptures.** Have you seen forms in your community? Are some of them sculptures? Tell about them.

Meet the Artist

Henry Moore's favorite subject to carve or sculpt was the human figure. At the same time, he studied nature to help with his projects. He once wrote that he saw "form and rhythm" in objects such as "pebbles, rocks, bones, trees, plants." Watch for another of Moore's large outdoor sculptures in this unit.

Lesson 1

Forms All Around

Forms are everywhere. You are a form. Forms have three dimensions. **Height** is the distance from top to bottom. **Width** is the distance from side to side. **Depth,** or thickness, is the distance from front to back.

How would you describe the three dimensions of the forms you see in these pictures?

Forms

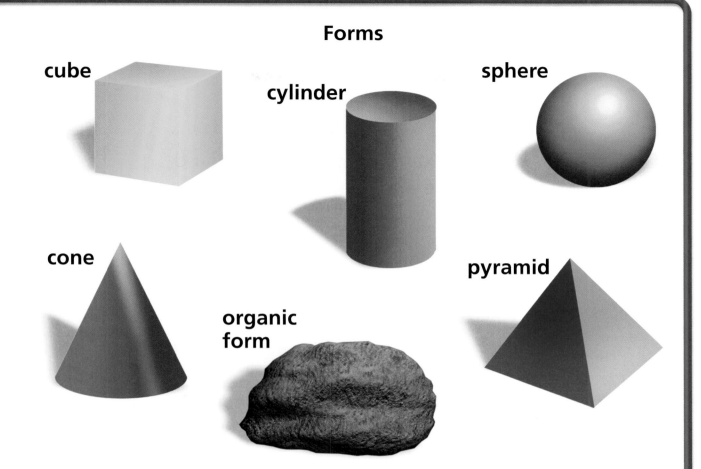

cube

cylinder

sphere

cone

organic form

pyramid

Like shapes, forms are geometric or organic. Look at the photographs on page 86. What geometric forms can you find? Name them.

Look around you. What geometric forms do you see? Choose one and point to its height, width, and depth.

How are forms different from shapes?

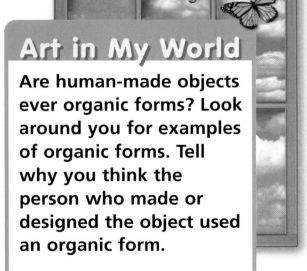

Art in My World

Are human-made objects ever organic forms? Look around you for examples of organic forms. Tell why you think the person who made or designed the object used an organic form.

Studio 1

Measure Forms

Look around you for examples of geometric and organic forms. Measure and draw them.

1 Measure the height, width, and depth of each form.

2 Draw each form.

Technique Tip

Forms can have different dimensions at different places. Measure at the highest, widest, and deepest place.

3 Record the dimensions of the forms on your drawings.

4 Show your work to a friend. Explain how you measured the forms.

Think Like an Artist

How is drawing a form different from drawing a shape?

Line Direction in Forms

These towers seem to be reaching up as towers of strength. Find the lines that go up and down. They are **vertical** lines.

Simon Rodia. *Watts Towers (seven towers total),* 1921–1954. Scrap metal and mosaic, height range 11 to 100 feet. Los Angeles, CA.

Claes Oldenburg and Coosje van Bruggen. *Spoonbridge with Cherry,* 1985-1988. Aluminum, stainless steel, paint, overall 354 by 618 by 162 inches. Courtesy Walker Art Center, Minneapolis, MN.

The lines of *Spoonbridge with Cherry* take your eye across, in a **horizontal** direction. Unlike the vertical lines in *Watts Towers,* horizontal lines often create a still, quiet feeling.

The lines in this field are slanted, or **diagonal.** Diagonal lines tend to create a busy or unsteady feeling.

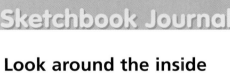

Sketchbook Journal

Look around the inside and the outside of your school for forms with vertical, diagonal, and horizontal lines. Draw what you see. How do different lines make you feel?

91

Make a Community

Make a diorama that shows a special form in your community. Include other forms, such as people, trees, and animals.

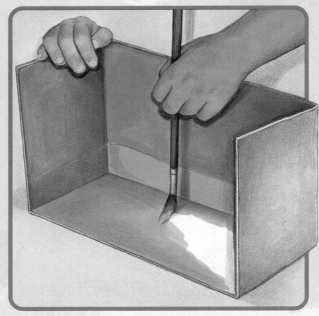

1 Paint the sky on the sides of your diorama.

2 Paint the ground. Think of forms to add to your community.

Technique Tip

You can join craft sticks with clay instead of glue. Press two sticks into a ball of clay.

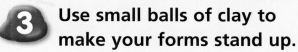

3 Use small balls of clay to make your forms stand up.

4 Make other forms that have different line directions.

Think Like an Artist

Do the forms in your diorama show vertical, horizontal, and diagonal lines? Describe them.

Proportion

Proportion shows how parts of objects relate to each other in size and position. This sculpture has unusual proportions. Does any part of the body look too big or too small? Describe what you see.

Artist unknown. *Votive Statue of Eannatum, Prince of Lagash,* 2600–2340 B.C. Alabaster, lapis lazuli, mother-of-pearl inlays, and modern bitumen inlays, 12 by 4½ by 4 inches. The Menil Collection, Houston, TX.

Artist unknown, Mexican. *Sculpture de Chupicuaro,* 7th–2nd century B.C. Terra-cotta, height 12¹⁄₁₀ inches. Musée du Quai Branly, Paris.

Some artists show proportion in unusual or interesting ways. Proportion can show emphasis and express thoughts or feelings. Describe the proportion in the sculpture above.

The figure's face and body show expression. They create a **mood,** or feeling. What feelings do you think they show?

Sketchbook Journal

Make sketches of ways your face and body can show happiness. Make other sketches of your face and body showing sadness. What moods do your expressions create? Write about them.

95

Make a Clay Model

Some days you may feel happy. Some days you may feel sad or even angry. Make a clay model of yourself expressing a feeling.

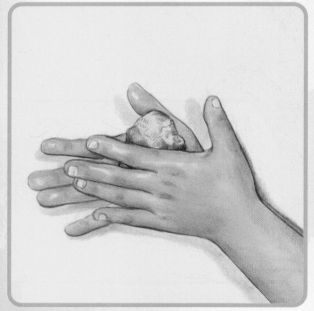

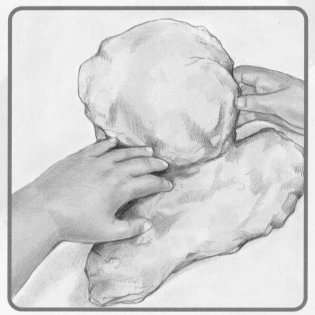

1 Prepare the clay for sculpting by pressing and squeezing it.

2 Mold the clay into a ball. Now you are ready to begin shaping a model.

Technique Tip

Clay is easier to form when it is warm. Squeeze and pinch the clay to warm it and make it soft.

3 Think about size proportion. Add facial features that express mood.

4 Use craft sticks or other tools to carve details into your sculpture.

Think Like an Artist

What does your sculpture's expression tell viewers about you?

Human Forms

Henry Moore. *Family Group,* 1951. Bronze, 59¼ by 26½ inches. Private collection.

These sculptures show feelings. What do you see?

Barbara Hepworth.
Figure for Landscape,
1960 (cast 1965). Bronze,
106½ by 53⅞ by 28⅜ inches.
Hirshhorn Museum and
Sculpture Garden,
Smithsonian Institution,
Washington, D.C. Gift of
Joseph H. Hirshhorn,
1966. Photograph by
Lee Stalsworth. 66.2450.

Describe the forms in each sculpture. How are the forms alike? How are they different? Which sculpture would you like to have at your school?

Both sculptures show human forms. Read both titles. How do they help you understand what the sculptures are about?

Sketchbook Journal

Why do you think the artists created their sculptures? Write your ideas. Tell how each sculpture makes you feel.

Pattern

An African king wore this mask. It was a **symbol** of power. The cowrie shells are symbols, too. They stand for wealth and ongoing life. How might it feel to wear this mask?

Artist unkown, Africa, Zaire, Western Kasai Province, Mweka Zone, Kuba People. *Mask of a mythic royal ancestor (Mukenga),* late 19th–early 20th century. Wood, beads, feathers, hair, cowrie shells, fiber, skin, metal, height 28 inches. The Art Institute of Chicago, Laura T. Magnuson Fund, X-Hautelet Collection. 1982.1504. Photograph by Robert Hashimoto © 1994, The Art Institute of Chicago. All rights reserved.

Artist unknown, Native American. *Bag.* ca. 1840-1860. Wool, silk, glass beads, and cotton, 6 by 6¼ inches. Fenimore Art Museum, Cooperstown, NY.

The African mask is covered with **patterns,** or repeated lines, shapes, forms, colors, or textures. What patterns do you see on the mask?

What patterns do you see on the beaded bag? What do the shapes on the bag make you think of?

Sketchbook Journal

Take your sketchbook outside. Look for patterns in natural forms. Find some repeated lines, shapes, and colors to draw.

Make a Pencil Pouch

Follow these steps to make a pencil pouch.
Decorate it with symbols and patterns.

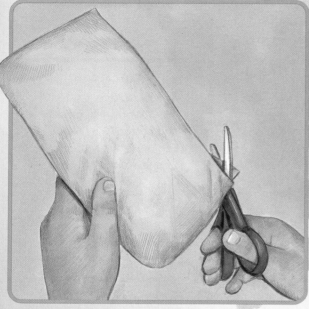

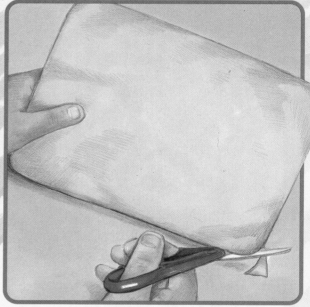

1 Draw and cut out a 4-by-9-inch rectangle. Round off the bottom corners.

2 Draw and cut out a 7-by-9-inch rectangle. Round all four corners.

Technique Tip

Wrinkle the two rectangles by squeezing them gently in your hands. This will give your pouch a crinkled effect.

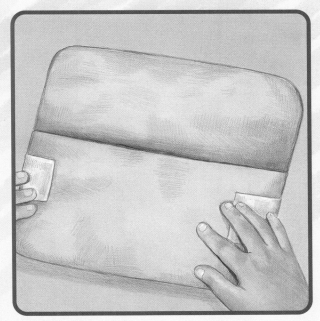

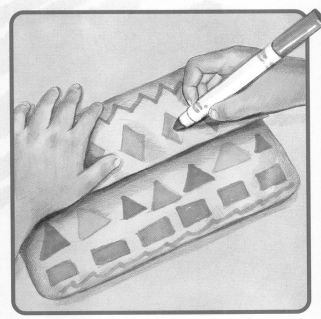

3 Use clear postage tape to attach the bottom and sides. Fold the flap over.

4 Use markers to draw a pattern with some symbols on the front and back.

Think Like an Artist

What do the symbols on your pouch stand for? Explain.

Ways of Sculpting

Someone created this sculpture about five thousand years ago. The artist made the **carving** by chipping away parts from a block of marble. Sculptors can make carvings from many kinds of materials, such as stone, marble, or wood.

Artist unknown.
Statuette of a Seated Harp Player, ca. 2800–2700 B.C. Marble, height 11½ inches. Metropolitan Museum of Art, New York.

How do you think the artist felt about music? Explain your answer.

Artist unknown.
Mayan Man and Woman, ca. A.D. 700. Buff clay with traces of color, 10½ by 5¾ by 3⅞ inches. Honolulu Academy of Arts Purchase, Charles Alfred Castle Memorial Fund, 1973. Photograph by Shuzo Uemoto.

How do this man and woman seem to feel about each other? Explain your answer.

Some artists sculpt by adding materials or attaching parts to a larger object. Long ago, an artist joined pieces of clay together to create the form shown on this page. Describe some of the parts of clay that have been added to this sculpture.

Research

Artists use special tools to make their sculptures. Look in an encyclopedia or other resource to find out about some of these tools.

Make a Foil Sculpture

Do you like baseball? How about swimming? Maybe soccer is your sport. Follow these steps to make a sculpture of a figure playing a sport.

1 Choose a sport or activity. Find pictures of people doing that activity.

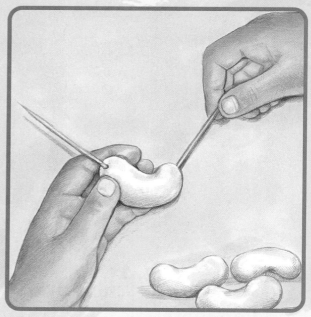

2 Use toothpicks and foam peanuts to form an active figure.

Technique Tip

Slide small parts of foam peanuts onto the toothpicks to add shape and bulk to your figure.

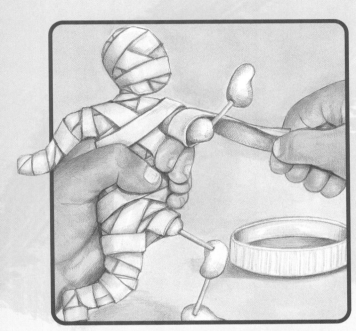

3 Tape the sections together. Then tape the sculpture to a jar lid.

4 Wrap the whole form in strips of aluminum foil.

Think Like an Artist

How can a viewer tell what sport your sculpture shows? Explain.

Found-Object Sculpture

What familiar items do you see in this sculpture? The artist used **found objects** to make it. It is an **assemblage** made by arranging and connecting a variety of objects.

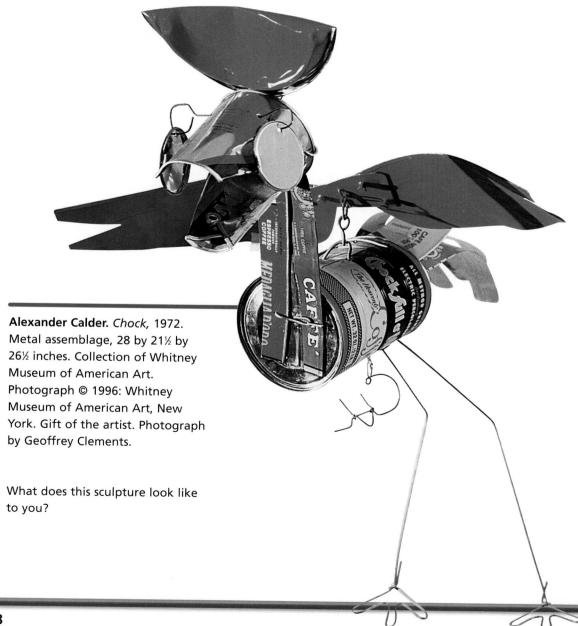

Alexander Calder. *Chock,* 1972. Metal assemblage, 28 by 21½ by 26½ inches. Collection of Whitney Museum of American Art. Photograph © 1996: Whitney Museum of American Art, New York. Gift of the artist. Photograph by Geoffrey Clements.

What does this sculpture look like to you?

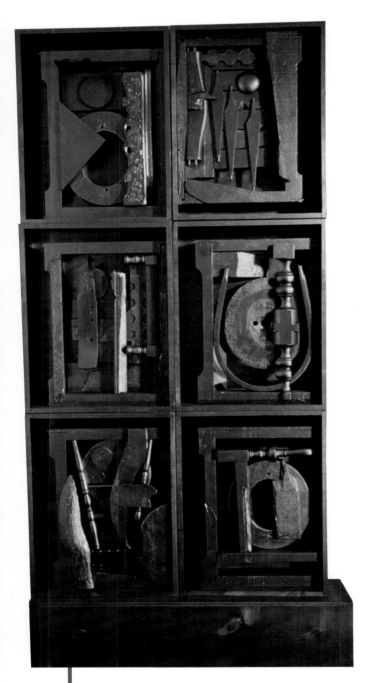

Found-object sculptures are made with things artists find. Often, the objects have been thrown away. How do you think the artist made this found-object sculpture? What objects do you recognize in it?

What found objects from home or school could you use to make a sculpture?

Louise Nevelson. *Moon Tower,* 1960–1961. Wood and found objects, painted gold. Private collection.

Sketchbook Journal

Think of some objects you may have seen that were thrown away. Draw a picture that shows them in a sculpture.

Studio 6

Use Found Objects

Work with a partner. Make something special with found objects. Follow these steps.

1 Choose a box lid or shallow box. Collect some found objects.

2 Try different ways of arranging your found objects in the box.

Technique Tip

Do not glue anything down until you are sure of your arrangement. Try out several arrangements for balance and proportion.

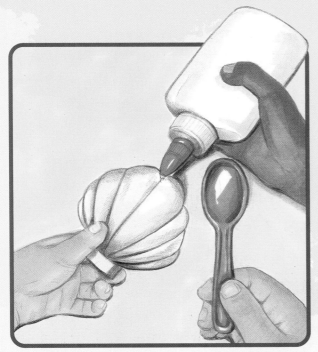

3 Decide on an arrangement. Glue down the objects.

4 Add several drops of glue to one color of tempera. Paint your artwork.

Think Like an Artist

What did you and your partner discuss as you decided where to glue your found objects?

Video Art

Suppose you are standing in front of *Internet Dweller: skaz.nine.msw.* You watch the flashing images on the television screens. You pay attention to one, then another. You are swept up in the lively personality of this sculpture.

The sculpture's creator, Nam June Paik, was among the first to create such art. He was born in North Korea. As a child, he studied piano. Later in Japan, he studied both art and music. Nam June Paik soon began experimenting with television sets. He used them to combine pictures and music into something new—video art.

Nam June Paik in his installation *Fish Flies on Sky,* 1976. Photograph by Peter Moore, © 1998 Estate of Peter Moore/Licensed by VAGA, New York.

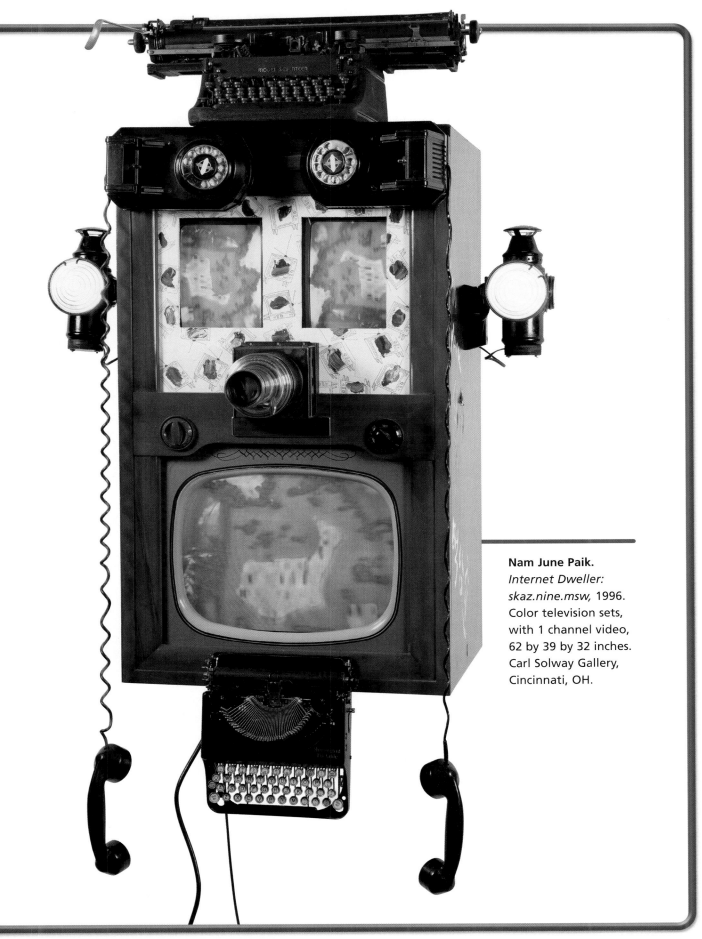

Nam June Paik.
Internet Dweller:
skaz.nine.msw, 1996.
Color television sets,
with 1 channel video,
62 by 39 by 32 inches.
Carl Solway Gallery,
Cincinnati, OH.

Build a Coil Pot

Think about how you could use a clay pot. Build one. Decorate it with a pattern of lines.

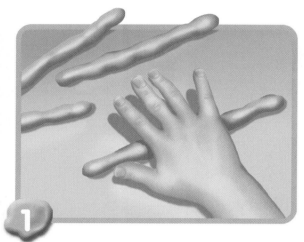

1 Roll out several coils about as thick as your index finger.

2 Make the base of your pot into a spiral form.

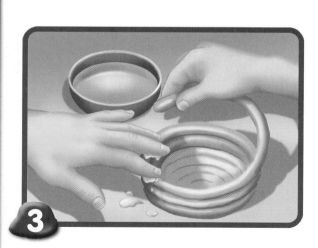

3 Score coils and apply slip as you build the pot upward.

4 Let your pot dry. Ask your teacher to fire it in a kiln. Decorate it.

Emily Ann, Age 8. *Stripes.* Clay and tempera paint.

Emily, Age 8. *Rainbow Pot.* Clay and tempera paint.

How could you use these coil pots made by other students?

Share Your Art

1. Name the kinds of lines you painted on your pot.

2. What was the best part about making your pot? Tell about it.

Think About Art

Read the art words. Then point to a picture that matches a word.

form	diagonal	pattern
vertical	proportion	sculpture

Write About Art

Write about your favorite sculpture. It can be one you made or one you have seen. Describe its form and lines.

Talk About Art

- Look at the artwork in your portfolio.
- Choose one you especially liked working on.
- Tell a friend why you liked working on it.
- Explain its form and any patterns or symbols you used.

Rev. J. L. Hunter. *Six Statues of Liberty,* 1985–1990. Carved found wood, tallest statue 22½ by 6½ by 2½ inches. Collection of Sally Griffiths, Dallas, TX.

Put It All Together

1. Describe the sculptures.

2. How are the proportions of the figures different?

3. What do you think the artist was saying?

4. Where would you display these sculptures?

Katsushika Hokusai. (Detail) *Paysans lavant leur cheval sous la cascade Yoshitsune (The Yoshitsune Horse-Washing Waterfall),* ca. 1831–1832. Woodcut, 15 by 10 inches. Collection of the Montreal Museum of Fine Arts.

Unit 4

Art, Then and Now

People have been making art for thousands of years. Then and now, artists have chosen people, places, and animals as their subjects. As the world changes, artworks change too. In this unit, you will see old and new ways of showing people, places, and animals.

Meet the Artist

Katsushika Hokusai may have made as many as thirty thousand drawings. He tried many different techniques during his long career. Look for more artwork by Hokusai in this unit.

Attributed to Katsushika Hokusai.
Untitled (Believed to be a self-portrait of Katsushika Hokusai).

Contrast

Artists show **contrast** with light and dark colors. The water lilies in this painting show clearly. The difference between the values makes the flowers stand out.

Claude Monet. *Bridge over a Pool of Water Lilies,* 1899. Oil on canvas, 36½ by 29 inches. The Metropolitan Museum of Art, New York.

This painting is more than one hundred years old. Why do you think artists continue to paint such scenes?

Vincent van Gogh. *Flowering Garden,* 1888. Oil on canvas, 28¾ by 36¼ inches. Private Collection, Zurich, Switzerland. On loan at Metropolitan Museum of Art, New York.

Monet used different tints and shades of color to make certain objects stand out. What do you see?

Now look at Van Gogh's painting. Name some contrasting color values.

Each artist has a special **style,** or way of creating. Monet's style includes cool, dark colors. How is Van Gogh's style different?

Sketchbook Journal

Take your sketchbook outdoors. Using colored pencils, draw a scene with light values against dark ones to make objects in your picture stand out.

Paint a Garden

Use tints and shades to create contrast in a painting. Think about your own style as you work.

1 Gather your art materials.

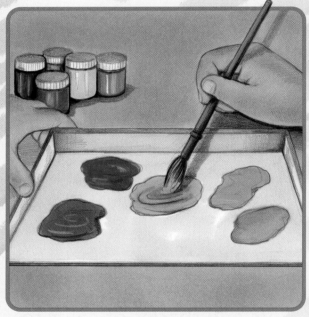

2 Mix colors for your stems and petals.

Technique Tip

To make leaves or petals contrast, paint them with tints. Paint spaces around them with darker shades.

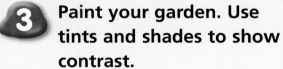 **3** Paint your garden. Use tints and shades to show contrast.

4 Use oil pastels or colored pencils to add details.

Think Like an Artist

How did you use contrasting values to make shapes stand out?

Portraits of People

An artwork that shows the likeness of a person or group of people is a **portrait.** Portraits can also show animals. Is this portrait old or new? How can you tell?

Rembrandt van Rijn.
Man in a Gold Helmet,
1650. Oil on canvas, 26¹⁄₁₀
by 19½ inches.
Gemäldegalerie,
Dahlem-Berlin, Germany.

Augusta Savage. *Gamin,* 1930. Bronze bust. Cleveland Museum of Art, Cleveland, OH.

Today, portraits are paintings, sculptures, or photographs. It seems that artists will always be interested in faces. Do you agree? Explain.

Some portraits show the profile, or side view, of a subject's face or body. Some show the subjects from the front. A portrait that shows the subject partly from the front and partly from the side is a **three-quarter view.** What kinds of portraits do you see in these artworks?

Long ago, many portraits were painted or sculpted.

Sketchbook Journal

Ask a friend to pose while you draw a portrait with a three-quarter view. Think about the facial expressions you might show.

Create a Clay Portrait

Use clay to form a portrait of a classmate. Work from a three-quarter view.

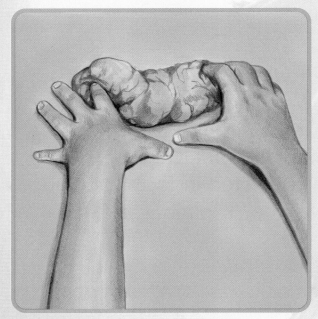

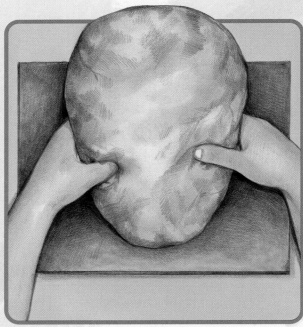

1 Press the clay against your work surface. Turn and press to create a ball.

2 Form the facial features using your fingers or some carving tools.

Technique Tip

Hollow out the inside of the head by scooping clay from the back. Cover the hole with a flat slab of clay.

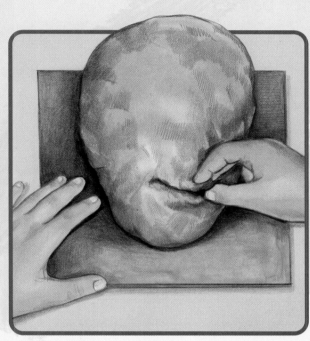

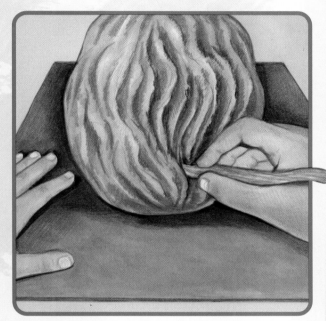

3 Arrange the features on your subject's face. Think about size and placement.

4 Use carving tools to add details or create texture.

Think Like an Artist

How is your sculpture like your subject's face? How is it different?

Portrait of an Artist

When Frida Kahlo painted this portrait of herself, she created a **self-portrait.** What can you learn about the artist from her painting?

Frida Kahlo. *Self-Portrait Dedicated to Leon Trotsky,* 1937. Oil on masonite, 30 by 24 inches. The National Museum of Women in the Arts, Washington, D.C. Gift of the Honorable Clare Boothe Luce.

Henri Rousseau. *I Myself-Portrait-Landscape,* 1890. Oil on canvas, 39⅜ by 31 inches. National Gallery, Prague, Czech Republic.

How can you tell that the man in this self-portrait was an artist?

Both of these paintings show their subjects from head to toe. They show a **full view.** Both paintings also show a **front view.** We see the subjects from the front. How is a front view different from a side view?

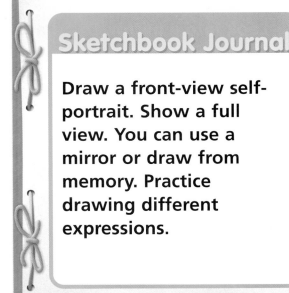

Sketchbook Journal

Draw a front-view self-portrait. Show a full view. You can use a mirror or draw from memory. Practice drawing different expressions.

Draw a Self-Portrait

Follow these steps to draw a self-portrait. Include a favorite object or symbol that says something about you.

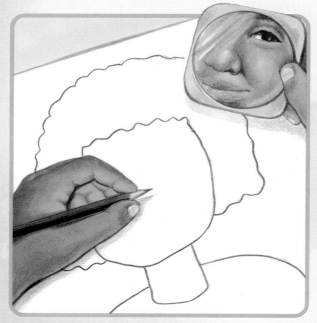

1 Look into a mirror. Draw a light sketch of your face and shoulder area.

2 Draw a special object or symbol in your self-portrait.

Technique Tip

On a human face, show the eyes halfway between the top of the head and the chin.

3 Mix some paints in values that show your eyes, hair, and other features.

4 Paint your self-portrait.

Think Like an Artist

Look at the self-portraits of some of your friends. Do you recognize each other from your self-portraits?

Look and Compare

River Scenes

Katsushika Hokusai. *Fuji from beneath Mannen Bridge in Fukagawa (Fukagawa mannenbashi shita), from the series Thirty-six Views of Mt. Fuji (Fugaku sanjurokkei),* ca. 1831–1834. Color woodcut, 9¾ by 14⅔ inches. Fine Arts Museums of San Francisco.

These rivers are in different places. The artworks were made at different times. Name some ways you can tell.

Claude Monet.
Reflections on the Thames River, 1899–1901. London. The Parliament. Oil on canvas, 31⅜ by 35⁹⁄₁₀ inches. Musée d'Orsay, Paris.

The artists used colors in different ways. Point to the contrasting colors. What colors do you think make the most interesting shapes in these artworks?

Notice the water in Hokusai's woodcut. Compare it to the water in Monet's painting. How does each artist's medium affect how the water looks?

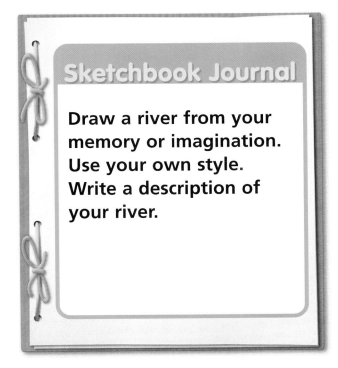

Sketchbook Journal

Draw a river from your memory or imagination. Use your own style. Write a description of your river.

Relief Sculptures

A **relief sculpture** has a raised design. This artwork was made from a sheet of gold and was pressed or hammered into a design. The process is called **embossing.**

Artist unknown. *Oxus: Gold Plaque of Standing Man,* 6th century. Gold. Private collection.

These ancient artworks come from different cultures. A **culture** is a set of ideas, beliefs, and values shared by a group of people. Artists often create in a style that tells something about their culture.

The mask on this page shows the face of a pharaoh, or king. How do you think people in this culture felt about their kings? What ideas do you think the relief sculptor had about weapons?

Art Fact

Tutankhamen was a young Egyptian king. His tomb lay nearly untouched for more than three thousand years. It was filled with gold jewelry, furniture, and weapons.

135

Make a Relief Sculpture

Make a relief sculpture of a favorite person or animal. Follow these steps.

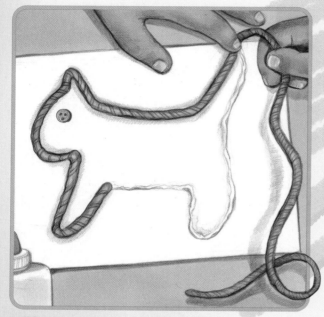

1 Draw the shape of your subject. Glue raised objects to your shape.

2 Mix glue and water. Brush the mixture onto the foil. Let it dry.

Technique Tip

Use the eraser end of a pencil to press the foil onto and around the objects. Try not to poke through the foil.

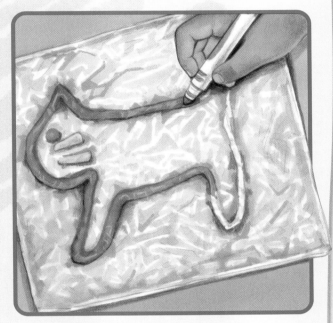

3 Press the foil over the sculpture. Fold it over the edges.

4 Use markers to outline interesting lines on your relief sculpture.

Think Like an Artist

What effect do the glued-down objects under the foil create?

Architecture

People have always needed homes. What other kinds of buildings do people need? The art of designing buildings is called **architecture.** In this photograph, what is new? What is old? Explain.

I. M. Pei, architect. *Entrance to the Louvre,* Paris, France.

The Louvre in Paris, France, is one of the largest art museums in the world.

Le Pont du Gard crosses the Gard River in southern France. The Romans built it in about 19 B.C. to carry water to the city of Nîmes. The bridge now carries traffic.

This landscaped area adds beauty to the Town Hall in Cognac, France.

Find the curved structures in the buildings and the bridge. These are called **arches.** Arches are often used for support.

The area around a building should look beautiful too. A landscape architect uses plants and trees to form a pleasing outdoor design. What plants would you use in a landscape design?

Art in My World

Think like an architect and plan a new entrance to your home. Will it have an arch? Will you use glass and geometric shapes, as in Pei's entrance to the Louvre? What materials will you use?

Studio 5

Plan an Animal Home

Design a home for an animal. Think about all of its needs. Follow these steps.

1 List the housing needs of a special animal.

2 Draw a home for the animal. Show what is inside.

Technique Tip

Keep in mind the animal's housing needs as you draw. Does it need to live with other animals or by itself?

3 Draw a garden outside the animal's home.

4 Add final details to your home design and garden.

Think Like an Artist

How does the home you designed suit the animal's needs?

Relief Prints

This artwork by Pablo Picasso is a **relief print.** To make the print, the artist created a raised image on a block of hard material. Notice the woman's facial features. What is unusual about them?

Pablo Picasso.
Jacqueline in a Black Hat, 1962. Linoleum cut in color, 24⅞ by 20½ inches. Courtesy of The Harvard Fogg Museum, Harvard University Art Museums, Cambridge, MA.

Katsushika Hokusai. *Woman Distracting a Child Whose Kite is Caught in a Tree,* ca. 1800. Color woodblock print, 7⅞ by 23⅔ inches. The Cleveland Museum of Art, Cleveland, OH.

To make a relief print, the artist carves a design into a **printing block.** With a **brayer,** or roller, the artist puts ink on the printing block and presses paper onto it. The result is a relief print.

The relief print on this page was made from a design carved into a block of wood. Point to the lines on the print that show where lines were carved away from the block.

Sketchbook Journal

The child in the print is flying a kite. Draw a picture of yourself doing a favorite outdoor activity. Include someone else in your drawing.

Make a Relief Print

What is your favorite outdoor activity? Show it in a relief print. Follow these steps.

1 Draw yourself playing your favorite outdoor game or sport.

2 Transfer the drawing to a meat tray by pressing the outlines with a pen.

Technique Tip

When you make prints, simple lines and shapes usually work best. You can add more lines to your block between printings.

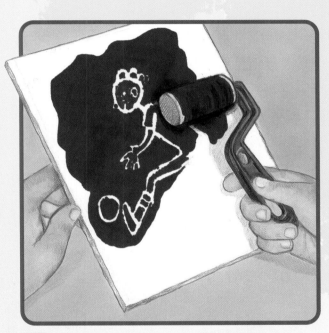

3 Roll just enough ink over your foam printing block to cover the surface.

4 Gently press paper over the foam. Carefully "pull the print."

Think Like an Artist

What does the relief print of yourself tell people about you?

News Photographs

Rodney Freeman tells stories, but not with words. He uses his camera instead. He is a photojournalist. He works for a newspaper. His job is to take photographs of the news.

Look for a photo-journalist like Freeman wherever an important or unusual event is happening. It might be an earthquake, a concert, a sporting event, or a frog-jumping contest.

You might see a photojournalist taking pictures at the mayor's office or at the site of a new school building.

Freeman wants people to experience an event as if they were there with him. He always hopes to tell the story of what is happening in front of his eyes and his lens. What story does Freeman tell with the photograph on page 147?

Rodney Freeman captures the news on camera.

Rodney Freeman. *On the Frontlines,* 2003. Digital photo.

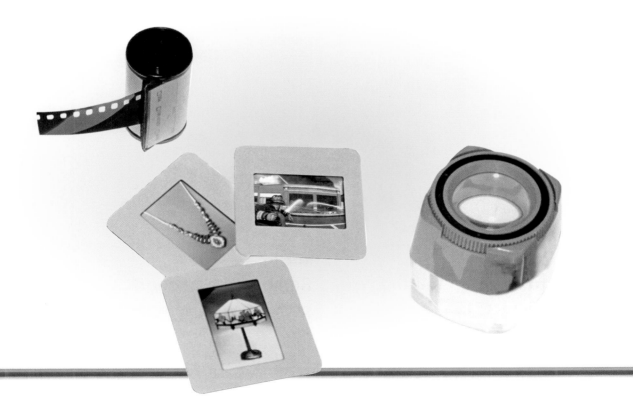

Mold a Portrait

Mold a portrait out of paper to hang on a wall. What person or animal will your portrait look like?

1 Shred newspaper into strips. Your teacher will blend them with water.

2 Scoop some pulp and squeeze out some of the water. Pat the pulp onto the side of a balloon.

3 Add pulp to build up features of the subject's face. Let the pulp dry.

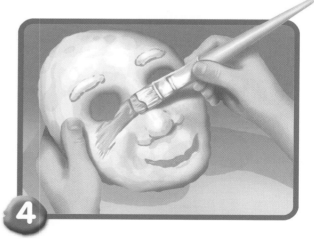

4 Remove the balloon. Paint your portrait with tempera paint.

Rebecca, Age 9. *Out of this World.* Shredded newsprint and tempera paint.

Casey, Age 8. *Flower.* Shredded newsprint and tempera paint.

Name three things you like about these molded paper portraits made by other students.

Share Your Art

1. What was the hardest part about making the portrait?

2. Does your portrait look like the person or animal? Tell how it is the same and different.

Think About Art

Read the art words. Match a picture to a word. A picture can match more than one word.

architecture   arches   front view
portrait   style

Write About Art

Describe the relief print you made in Studio 6. Summarize how you made it. Write about some relief prints your friends made.

Talk About Art

- Look through your portfolio.
- Choose an artwork that makes you proud.
- Tell a friend why you chose this artwork.
- Use the words *style* and *contrast* as you talk about your artwork.

Akati Ekplékendo. *Sculpture Dedicated to Gou, God of Iron and War,* ca. 1858. Iron, 64⅓ inches. Musée National d'Histoire Naturelle, Musée de l'Homme. Photo © Musée du Quai Branly, Paris.

Put It All Together

1. Describe what the subject is doing.

2. How did the artist show unity and variety?

3. What message do you think the artist was trying to convey?

4. What interests you most about the sculpture? Why?

David Hockney. *Mother, Los Angeles, Dec. 1982,* 1982. Photographic collage,
53 by 39 inches. © David Hockney.

Artists and Expression

People show their thoughts, ideas, and feelings through many art forms. Writing and dancing are two forms of expression. People also **express** themselves through visual arts, such as painting and sculpture. Cameras and computers provide other ways to express ideas. What are some of *your* favorite ways to express yourself?

Meet the Artist

DAVID HOCKNEY

ng with a Camera

David Hockney is a British artist who now lives in California. Most of his artworks show himself, his friends, and places he has traveled.

Hockney has expressed himself through paint, photography, and computers. Look for other artworks by David Hockney later in this unit.

Quilts as Expression

Whoever heard of dancing in a museum? The people in this painting are at an **exhibition,** or public showing, of artworks. What idea do you think Faith Ringgold expresses in this artwork? What details do you notice in the fabric border?

Faith Ringgold. *The French Collection Part I, #1: Dancing at the Louvre,* 1991. Acrylic on canvas with border, 73½ by 80½ inches. Private collection.
© 1991 Faith Ringgold

The border of Ringgold's painting shows a **quilt.** Like many of her artworks, it is a **story quilt.** What story does the quilt tell?

The image on this page shows a quilt too. Many artists worked together to make it. Each sewed a block, or a section. Then they sewed all the blocks together. Look at the title and date of the quilt. What do you think it celebrates?

San Antonio Needlework Guild. *Bicentennial Quilt,* 1976. Appliquéd cotton, 107 by 73 inches. Courtesy of The Witte Museum, San Antonio, TX.

What objects do you see in the blocks of this quilt?

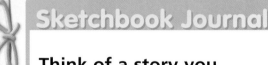

Sketchbook Journal

Think of a story you want to share. Draw a story quilt with line, shape, and color. Will you add words to your story quilt?

155

Make a Story Quilt

Work with your classmates to make a story quilt. Agree on a story. Then decide what part of the story each of you will tell. Follow these steps.

1 Cut square blocks from scraps of fabric or wallpaper.

2 Glue the squares to a sheet of poster board or tag board.

Technique Tip

Before you glue, arrange the squares in a pleasing way. For example, you may want to place the squares in a pattern.

3 Use markers to help tell your story.

4 Attach your part of the quilt to a bulletin board for a class display.

Think Like an Artist

What part of the story does your artwork tell?

Expression and Style

Artists use different styles when expressing ideas. Style is an artist's own way of creating an artwork. How would you describe Gabriele Münter's style? Münter shared this style with other **German Expressionists.** This group of artists painted in Germany about one hundred years ago.

Gabriele Münter. *Jawlensky and Werefkin,* 1908–1909. Oil on cardboard, 12⅞ by 17½ inches. Städtische Galerie im Lenbachhaus, Munich. © 1998 Artists Rights Society (ARS), New York/VG Bild Kunst, Bonn. Image GMS 655.

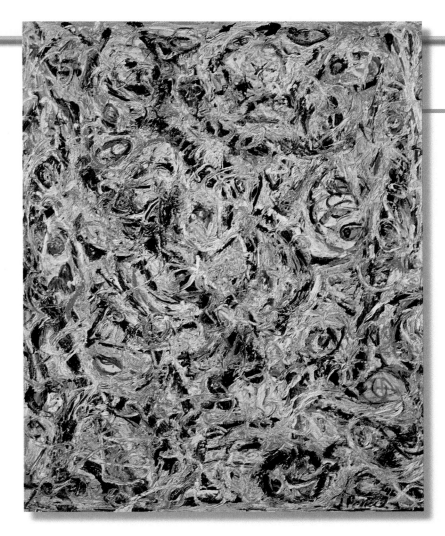

Jackson Pollock. *Eyes in the Heat,* 1946. Oil (and enamel?) on canvas, 54 by 43 inches. Peggy Guggenheim Collection, Venice, Italy.

Jackson Pollock was an **Abstract Expressionist.** These artists lived in the United States. They painted boldly and freely. They even dripped or splattered paint on large canvases.

Pollock's painting is also in a **nonobjective** style. It does not show recognizable objects. How is it different from Münter's painting?

Sketchbook Journal

Draw a picture that shows you expressing yourself in your favorite way. How do you feel when you are expressing yourself? List words that describe your feelings.

Paint with Expression

The German Expressionists used bright colors to create lines and abstract shapes. Paint a picture in the same style. Follow these steps.

1 Think of an outdoor scene that you would like to paint.

2 Draw the scene. Show some flat shapes.

Technique Tip

Place tints and shades next to each other. The contrast wil make your shapes stand out.

3 Paint the scene with bright colors. Let it dry.

4 Use black to outline some of your shapes.

Think Like an Artist

In what ways is your artwork like that of a German Expressionist?

Cameras and Expression

Photographers take pictures to capture a special image or a moment in time. What kinds of lines did the photographer of this bridge capture?

Margaret Bourke-White. *The George Washington Bridge,* 1933. Silver print photograph, 12⅜ by 8¾ inches. Boston Museum of Fine Arts, Charles Amos Cummings Fund, 1988 1988.2.

Joe McNally. *Bolshoi Ballerina*, 1997. Color photograph. Collection of the artist.
© Joe McNally.

The artist who took this **photograph** planned the moment he wanted to capture. What mood does the photograph express?

Many photographers today use **digital cameras.** These cameras record images without film. The pictures they take can be printed, emailed, or posted on a Web site.

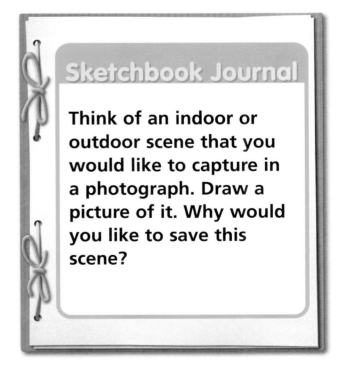

Sketchbook Journal

Think of an indoor or outdoor scene that you would like to capture in a photograph. Draw a picture of it. Why would you like to save this scene?

Make Photocopy Art

Use the "camera" inside a photocopy machine to take pictures. Follow these steps.

1 On your desk, make a pleasing arrangement of several flat objects.

2 Place your arrangement face down on the glass of a photocopy machine.

Technique Tip

Think about how you will arrange the items to fill the space. Try to imagine the lines and shapes the objects will create.

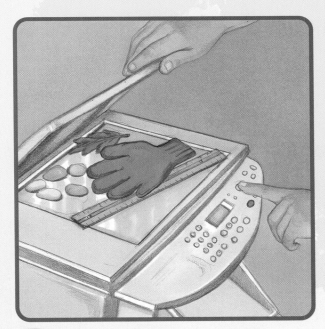

3 Lower the cover of the machine. Make a copy.

4 Use markers to color your artwork.

Think Like an Artist

How did adding color to your photocopy change it?

Places and Feelings

This artist used lines, shapes, and colors to express his thoughts and feelings about a familiar road. Follow the lines with your finger. Where do they take you? How would you use elements of art to show a road that *you* know?

David Hockney. *Mulholland Drive: The Road to the Studio,* 1980. Acrylic on canvas, 86 by 243 inches. Los Angeles County Museum of Art, purchased with funds provided by the F. Patrick Burnes Bequest. © David Hockney. Photograph © 1996, Museum Associates, Los Angeles County Museum of Art. All rights reserved.

Friedensreich Hundertwasser. *540 House and Spiral in the Rain,* 1962. Color lithograph, approximately 9 by 12 inches (image) and 14 by 19 inches (sheet). Purchase from Galerie Aenne Abels, Cologne. © Gruener Janura AG, Glarus, Switzerland.

The artwork above expresses another artist's thoughts and feelings about a place. What kinds of lines, shapes, and colors did each artist use? How are these two artworks different?

Both artworks are abstract. Where do you see flat shapes that remind you of familiar objects?

Sketchbook Journal

Draw a familiar road or place. Include many lines and shapes. If you like, use an abstract style in your drawing. How does your artwork show your feelings about the road or place?

Photographs in Art

This artwork may look unlike most photographs you have seen. The artist made it by combining parts of different photographs. This type of artwork is called a **photomontage.** What symbols did the artist include?

David Hockney. *Pearblossom Hwy., 11–18 April 1986, (Second Version),* 1986. Photographic collage, 71½ by 107 inches. The J. Paul Getty Museum, Los Angeles, CA. © David Hockney.

Romare Bearden. *Return of the Prodigal Son,* 1967. Mixed media and collage on canvas, 50¼ by 60 inches. Albright-Knox Art Gallery, Buffalo, NY. © Romare Bearden Foundation/Licensed by VAGA, New York, NY.

Romare Bearden created this photomontage with photographs and paper cut into different shapes. How did he show proportion?

Some artists create their photomontages in a studio. A **studio** is a place where an artist makes art. What special place can you use as a studio?

Studio 4

Make a Photomontage

Think of some symbols. Use them in a photomontage. Follow these steps.

1 Draw some symbols for your artwork.

2 Color symbols with your favorite color scheme. Cut them out.

Technique Tip

Before you begin coloring, decide on a color scheme. You may want to use warm or cool colors.

3 Arrange the symbols on poster board. Add pictures and shapes from magazines.

4 Choose the arrangement you like best. Glue down the symbols and pictures.

Think Like an Artist

Do you like the final arrangement of your photomontage? Explain.

Computer Art

Look closely at this print by Karen Guzak to find many layers of lines and shapes. Some were drawn on a computer. Others were drawn by hand. Point to places where lines and shapes overlap.

Karen Guzak. *Range Finder,* 1987. Lithograph, 22 by 29 inches. Davidson Galleries, Seattle, WA.

Some artists *create* art on computer. Other artists use computer technology to alter or add special effects to art they create by hand.

Computer technology is another medium some artists use to express themselves. This artist is using a computer to draw. Artists can also "paint," cut and paste, and print images using a computer.

What ideas would you like to express with computer art?

Sketchbook Journal

Think of a design you could make on a computer. Draw some lines and shapes you would like to use in your computer design.

Draw on a Computer

With a computer drawing program, create a nonobjective design. Print it out on a computer printer. Then follow these steps.

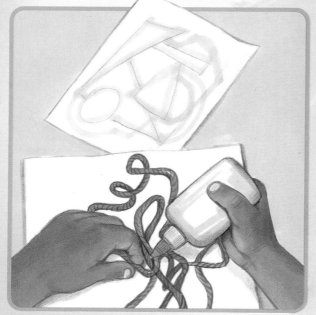

1 Glue yarn onto a cardboard printing plate to show rhythm.

2 Paint the shapes inside your yarn design with tempera.

Technique Tip

Be sure to save the design you created on a computer. You may want to print it out again.

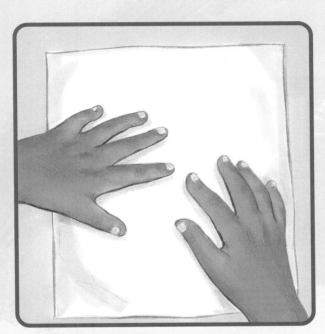

3 Gently press the computer print, face down, onto the wet printing plate.

4 Pull the print. Add more paint and print again.

Think Like an Artist

What kinds of lines does your print have?
Describe them to someone.

Landscape Art

People visit parks and gardens to relax, to exercise, and for many other reasons. Think of the most beautiful garden you have ever seen. What made it special?

Isamu Taniguchi. Zilker Gardens in Austin, Texas.

What mood does this Japanese garden create?

For this garden in England, the landscape architect lined a walking path with brightly colored flowers in plots of different shapes and sizes.

Landscape architecture is the planning and design of outdoor spaces, such as parks. The artists, or landscape architects, plan how to arrange plants, water, paths, and grassy areas. They must think about how the place will look during each season.

The photograph on this page shows an example of landscape architecture. Would you like to visit this place? Explain.

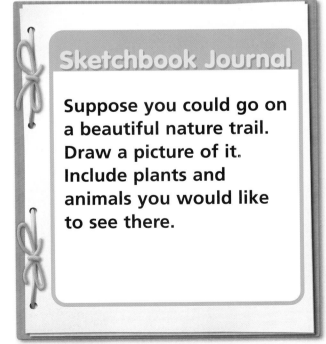

Sketchbook Journal

Suppose you could go on a beautiful nature trail. Draw a picture of it. Include plants and animals you would like to see there.

Design a School Garden

Design a garden where you and your friends can read, talk, or eat lunch. Follow these steps.

1 Work in a group to make a list of outdoor plants that grow in your area.

2 Draw and color the plant shapes. Then cut them out.

Technique Tip

Think of the size proportions of your plants. Put larger plants near the back or center of your garden.

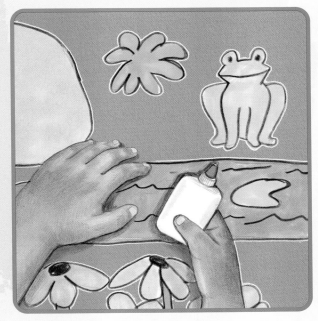

3 Draw and color special features for your garden. Cut them out.

4 Arrange the shapes on craft paper. Glue them down.

Think Like an Artist

How did the colors of the plants you chose affect your garden?

Art Galleries

How does Bernice Steinbaum help artists?

What do artists do with artworks that they have created? Sometimes artists want to sell them in an art gallery.

Bernice Steinbaum owns an art gallery in which artists show and sell their artworks. In her gallery, she exhibits artworks made by artists from different cultures. She feels strongly about supporting women artists and artists of color, including those whose backgrounds are African, Asian, Latino, and Native American.

One of Steinbaum's goals is to make artists and their art more public. By putting

Bernice Steinbaum's gallery in Miami, Florida

art on display, she believes more people will learn to appreciate it.

Steinbaum also likes to exhibit unusual artworks in her gallery. Such artworks might show an unusual style or include unusual media. Steinbaum values her gallery as a place where ideas are exchanged. She changes the displays often to make sure people see new ideas each time they visit.

Would you like to own an art gallery? What kind of art would you choose to show there?

Express Yourself

Work with paint and other media to express your thoughts and feelings as an artist. Follow these steps.

1 Make small puddles on paper with thinned paint. Blow the puddles with a straw.

2 Draw and color several pictures. Cut out the drawings and some magazine photographs.

3 Arrange the pictures on the dry blow painting. Show a design that pleases you.

4 Glue down the images.

Justin, Age 9. *Wild Forest.* Collage.

How is your multimedia painting similar to the ones made by other students? How is it different?

Wesley, Age 8. *The Sea.* Collage.

Share Your Art

1. Point to the different media you used in your artwork.

2. Is there anything you would do differently the next time you make a multimedia painting? Tell about it.

Unit Review

Think About Art

Read the art words. Then point to a picture that matches a word. A picture can go with more than one word.

photograph   landscape architecture   quilt
exhibition   nonobjective

Write About Art

What photographs of your surroundings would look good in a photomontage? Write about them.

Talk About Art

- Look at the artworks you created for this unit.
- Choose your favorite artwork.
- Tell a friend why you like it or why you enjoyed making it.

Mark Tobey. *Echoes of Broadway,* 1964. Tempera on paper, 52¼ by 25½ inches. Dallas Museum of Art. Gift of the artist. 1967.18. © 1997 Artists Rights Society (ARS), New York/Pro Litteris, Zurich.

Put It All Together

1. How did this artist use line, shape, and color?

2. What makes this artwork nonobjective?

3. What mood does the artwork express?

4. Do you think the artist succeeded in expressing his thoughts and feelings about a busy street in a busy city? Explain.

Nancy Graves. *Wheelabout,* 1985. Bronze with stainless steel and polyurethane paint, 92½ by 70 by 32½ inches. Collection of the Modern Art Museum of Fort Worth, Fort Worth, TX. © 2003 Nancy Graves Foundation/Licensed by VAGA, New York.

A World of Art

People all over the world create art. Some artworks, such as telephones and furniture, are useful. Some artworks are both useful and fun. Look at Nancy Graves's artwork. Is it useful or is it fun?

Meet the Artist

Nancy Graves worked in many media. She created drawings, paintings, sculptures, and even films. Graves was also interested in science. She liked to learn about living things. How does this artwork show her interest? Look for another sculpture by Nancy Graves later in the unit.

Fiber Artworks

Children in different parts of the world wear clothes like those shown here. They are made from **fibers,** or the threads that make up yarn, string, and different kinds of fabric. What are you wearing that is made from fibers?

Artist unknown, Amusgo people, Mexico. *Boy's Outfit: Shirt and Pants,* 1971. Handspun cotton. Museum of International Folk Art Foundation, Museum of International Folk Art, Santa Fe, NM. Photo by Blair Clark.

Berl and Sarah Krasner Scolnik (Ukraine). *Girl's Outfit: Skirt, Underskirt, Apron, and Sash*, 1910. Cotton, linen, and wool. Museum of International Folk Art, Santa Fe, NM. Photo by Blair Clark.

Artist unknown, Moroccan. *Child's Burnoose,* 1963. Wool and silk. Museum of International Folk Art, Santa Fe, NM. Photo by Blair Clark.

Artist unknown, Indian. *Child's Dress,* early 20th century. Silk and metal thread. Museum of International Folk Art Foundation, Museum of International Folk Art, Santa Fe, NM. Photo by Blair Clark.

Some artists **weave** fabric, or cloth, on a loom. The frame-like **loom** holds one set of fibers while the artist weaves another set over and under.

Point to different fabrics on these pages. How is your clothing like these outfits from other countries?

Sketchbook Journal

Think of a fabric you would like to weave. Draw a picture of an outfit made from the fabric. Write a sentence about where you would wear your newly woven outfit.

Studio 1

Make a Bookmark

Your favorite book deserves a hand-made bookmark. Follow these steps to make one.

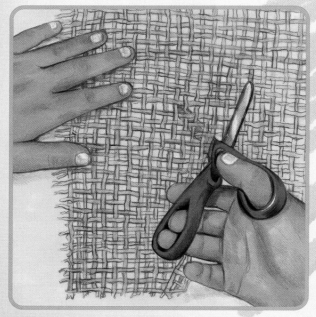

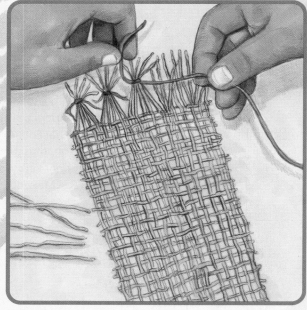

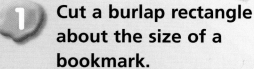
1 Cut a burlap rectangle about the size of a bookmark.

2 Pull away five horizontal threads. Tie groups of five vertical threads.

Technique Tip

To keep the bookmark from unraveling, put small drops of white glue along the top and bottom horizontal rows. Let it dry.

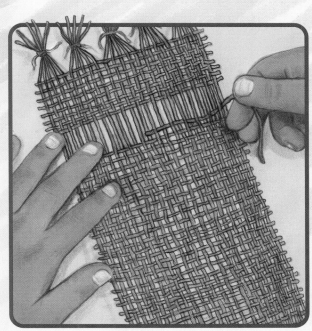

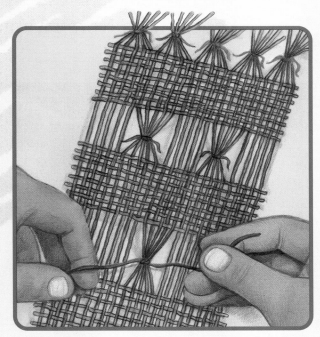

3 Count down eight strands. Remove several strands. Count eight, and so on.

4 Tie together some bunches of vertical strands in the middle of the bookmark.

Think Like an Artist

What parts of your bookmark show patterns? How will you use it?

Baskets as Art

Fishermen in some parts of Japan use woven baskets, such as this one, to catch fish. Fish swim into the baskets to eat the bait. A small gate inside keeps them from swimming out.

Hiroshima Kazuo. *Japanese Fishtrap Basket,* 1986. Bamboo, rope, metal wire, and string, 19⅞ by 19⅞ inches. National Museum of Natural History, Smithsonian Institution, Washington, D.C. © 2003 Smithsonian Institution.

Elizabeth Conrad Hickox. *Fancy Basket,* ca. 1918. Roots and bear grass, 4¾ by 3¾ inches. Karuk, Klamath River, northern California. Fenimore Art Museum, Cooperstown, NY.

These baskets were made by weaving. Point to the vertical fibers on each basket. These are called the **warp.** Now point to the horizontal fibers. They are called the **weft.** The weft is woven over and under the warp.

Basket weaving is an ancient art. People made baskets to hold food and water. How do people today use baskets?

Sketchbook Journal

Draw a design for a basket you might weave. What fibers would you use? Would your basket be useful, for decoration, or both? Write several sentences that describe your basket.

Create a Weaving

Follow these steps to make a weaving on a loom. What patterns and textures would you like to show in your weaving?

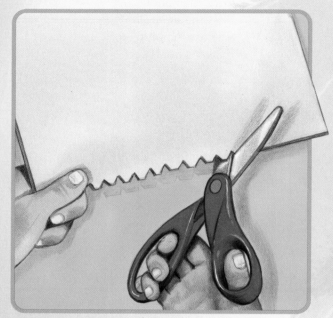

1 Cut a sheet of cardboard for your loom. Notch the top and bottom edges.

2 Hook yarn around each notch, working from top to bottom to top, and so on.

Technique Tip

Set your first row of weft threads at least an inch from the end of the loom. This will leave room for tying knots at the end.

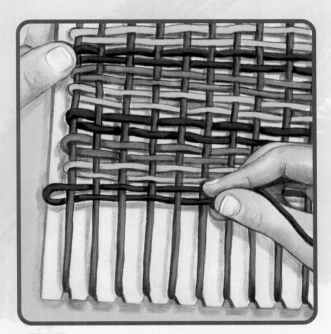

3 Weave the weft threads over and under the warp threads in a pattern.

4 Unhook the warp threads and knot the ends.

Think Like an Artist

Do you like the colors and textures you used in your weaving? Explain. Describe the best part of your weaving.

Batik as Fiber Art

Artists colored the fabrics on these pages with liquid stains called **dye.** They put a **resist,** such as wax, on the areas of the fabrics they did not want to be dyed. The resist caused the dye to roll off. Later they removed the resist from the fabrics. This process of dyeing is called **batik.** Point to the areas of the fabrics that were coated with resist.

Artist unknown, Central Java, possibly Surakarta. *Cotton Batik Skirt Cloth,* 1930s. Victoria and Albert Museum, London.

This batik was made on an island in the Indian Ocean.

Lawrence Wanga
Oniameo. *Dancing
Giraffes.* Batik on cut
muslin, 38 by 36 inches.
Private collection.

The artist of this batik
is from Kenya in Africa.

Look at the giraffes. Let your eye move from one giraffe's neck to the next. A feeling of motion, or **rhythm,** comes from the repeated elements of art that the artist used. Find repeated lines, colors, and shapes in *Dancing Giraffes* that show rhythm.

Sketchbook Journal

Draw a pattern for a batik you would like to make. Repeat lines, colors, and shapes to show rhythm. Where will you use resist? Write a sentence that describes your batik.

Studio 3

Create a Batik

Follow these steps to create a batik. What colors and patterns will you show on your fabric?

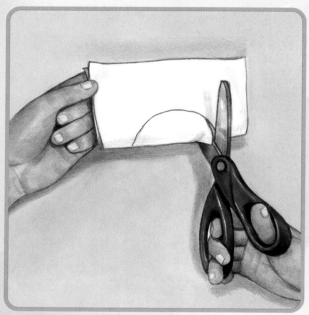

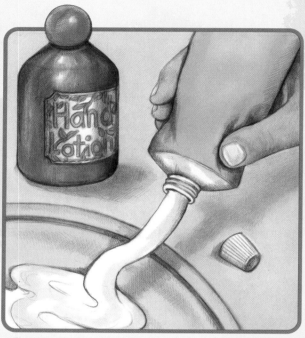

1 Fold a small sheet of paper in half. Cut a simple stencil from it.

2 Make a resist of toothpaste and hand lotion. Brush it through the stencil.

Technique Tip

Use darker colors of paint. This will help make your resist pattern stand out.

3 Move the stencil and repeat the process to make a pattern. Let dry.

4 Brush the entire cloth with tempera paints. After it dries, wash out the resist.

Think Like an Artist

How is your batik different from your classmates' artworks? In what ways did you or your classmates show rhythm?

Sculptures

Nancy Graves.
Immovable Iconography,
1990. Bronze, steel and
enamel, 23 by 22 by 12
inches. Kemper Museum
of Contemporary Art,
Kansas City, MO.
© 2003 Nancy Graves
Foundation/Licensed
by VAGA, New York.

Artworks can represent, or stand for, different
ideas. What do you think these artworks
represent? Point to the positive space in each
sculpture. Why do you think these two artists
created their sculptures?

Marisol Escobar.
President Charles DeGaulle, 1967. Mixed media with wood, plaster, and mirror, 107¼ by 86¼ by 31⅞ inches. Smithsonian American Art Museum, Washington, D.C.

Compare the colors, lines, and forms in the sculptures. What kind of balance does each artist show?

If you could borrow one of the sculptures to show at your school, which one would you choose? Where would you place it? Explain why.

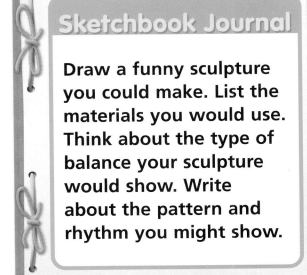

Sketchbook Journal

Draw a funny sculpture you could make. List the materials you would use. Think about the type of balance your sculpture would show. Write about the pattern and rhythm you might show.

Folk Art

These small figures were made by artists from Peru. The figures are examples of **folk art.** Folk artists do not usually learn to make art in school. Some learn to make art from family members, as their ancestors did. Others teach themselves how to draw, paint, or sculpt.

Artist unknown.
Peruvian Figures.
Painted ceramic, 5 by 2 by 1 inches. Private collection.

Artist unknown, Guanajuato, Mexico. *Horse Toy*, ca. 1960. Painted papier-mâché, height 14¾ inches. Museum of International Folk Art, Santa Fe, NM.

This toy horse is made of **papier-mâché.** Papier-mâché artists start with an armature. An **armature** is a frame made of wire or other materials. The artists cover the armatures with strips of paper soaked in watery paste. They mold the paper to the form and let it dry. Finally the artists add color and pattern with paint.

Sketchbook Journal

Draw a picture of an artwork about an animal. Use your imagination. Write a description of your animal. Tell about the size, forms, colors, patterns, and rhythm it has.

Make Papier-Mâché Art

Follow these steps to make a papier-mâché creature. What forms will you use?

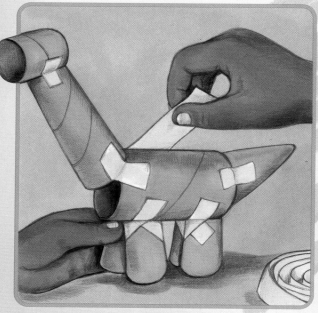

1 Make an armature from cardboard tubes, wadded newspaper, or wire.

2 Dip newspaper strips in papier-mâché paste. Apply layers over your armature.

Technique Tip

Let each layer of newspaper strips dry before adding a new one. Apply at least three layers.

3 Paint your creature with tempera paints.

4 Add details with buttons, yarn, and other materials.

Think Like an Artist

What do you like best about your papier-mâché sculpture? Tell why. Give your creature a name.

Graphic Design

This poster is an example of **graphic design.** Graphic designs can be signs in stores. You can also see them on books and on television. They show and tell about ideas using pictures and words. What ideas does this poster show?

Marvin Mattelson, illustrator. *Untitled,* 1982. Subway poster designed by the School of Visual Arts. Richard Wilde and Silas H. Rhodes, Art Directors; William J. Kobasz, Designer; Dee Ito, Copywriter. Courtesy of the School of Visual Arts, New York.

To be good is not enough, when you dream of being great.

SCHOOL OF VISUAL ARTS

Animated still from the movie *Ice Age*

What are your favorite book **illustrations?** These artworks help tell stories. Graphic design artists, called **illustrators,** often make them. Many illustrations are created on a computer.

The **computer-aided animation** above shows one image from an animated film. The image was made on a computer.

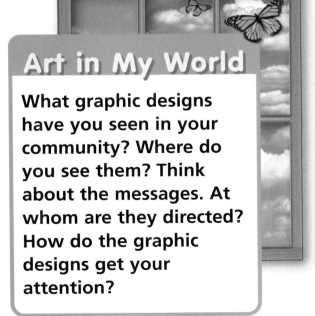

Art in My World

What graphic designs have you seen in your community? Where do you see them? Think about the messages. At whom are they directed? How do the graphic designs get your attention?

Studio 5

Create a Poster

Think of a message you would like to post in your community. Follow these steps to make a poster for it.

1 Make drawings of ideas for your poster. Include pictures and words.

2 On poster board, make a final drawing of your best idea.

Technique Tip

Put important words on your poster. Make the words large so they can be seen from across the room or down the sidewalk.

3 Complete your poster with construction paper, paint, and markers.

4 Get permission to hang your poster where many people can see it.

Think Like an Artist

How do the words and pictures in your poster send your message? How did you arrange the composition to create your poster?

Industrial Design as Art

Does this clock look like others you have seen? How is it the same and different? Interesting designs for objects such as clocks, chairs, shoes, and telephones are examples of **industrial design.** Look for other examples of industrial design in your classroom.

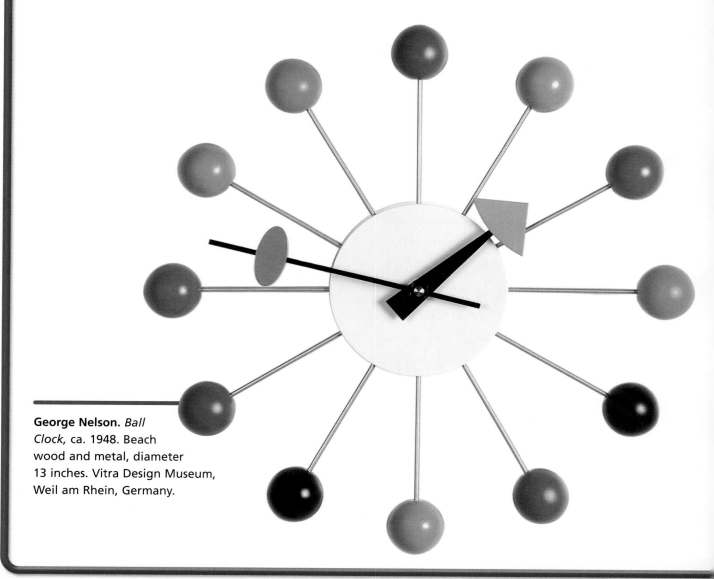

George Nelson. *Ball Clock,* ca. 1948. Beach wood and metal, diameter 13 inches. Vitra Design Museum, Weil am Rhein, Germany.

Philippe Starck. *LA MARIE Chair*, 2000. Transparent or batch-dyed polycarbonate, 34 by 15½ by 16 inches. LA MARIE by Kartell, design Philippe Starck.

Why do you think the designer chose these colors for the chairs?

Industrial designers plan objects such as the clock and these chairs. These artists want the objects they design to be safe, useful, and attractive. The objects are made in a factory for people to buy and use.

What other objects that you use were planned by industrial designers?

Sketchbook Journal

Draw an industrial design for a new telephone. What special features will it have? Write a telephone conversation about the new telephone and its design.

Design a New Object

Pretend you are an industrial designer. Make a collage showing a design for a new object. What will it be used for?

1 Cut out pictures of objects that show industrial design.

2 Use parts of the pictures to form a new invention or a new design.

Technique Tip

Think about the lines of your new object. Will it be slim and sleek? Will it be square and sturdy? Use lines that are best for its purpose.

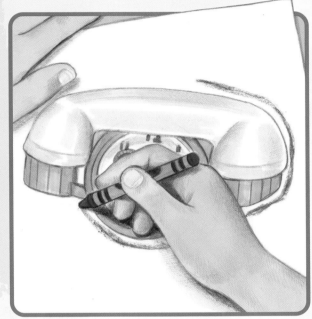

3 Glue the arrangement onto poster board.

4 Add details with crayons or colored pencils. Think of a name for your object.

Think Like an Artist

How will your new object be used? Who will purchase it?

Living Spaces

Cecil Hayes is an artist who designs living spaces. She is an interior designer. Some interior designers create pleasing office spaces for workers. Others design restful hotel rooms. Some even design elegant eating places. Cecil Hayes designs room interiors for people's homes.

Interior designers like Hayes must think about how a room will be used. They must also think about what colors and styles the people using the room like. Hayes shows people samples of paints, fabrics, carpets, and furniture. She shows them sketches of how the room will look. The people choose the colors and other items they like best. Then Hayes and her team redecorate the room based on the owners' choices and Hayes's own artistic ideas.

Think of your favorite room at home or school. Does the room make you feel happy? Does it make you feel calm and cozy? Maybe it makes you feel full of energy. What is it about the room that makes you feel that way?

Cecil Hayes designs living spaces that make people happy.

Cecil Hayes. *Painter's Paradise,* 1992. 20 by 18 feet. Private residence, Palm Beach, FL. Photo © 1992 by Dan Forer.

What colors, lines, and patterns did Hayes choose for this room?

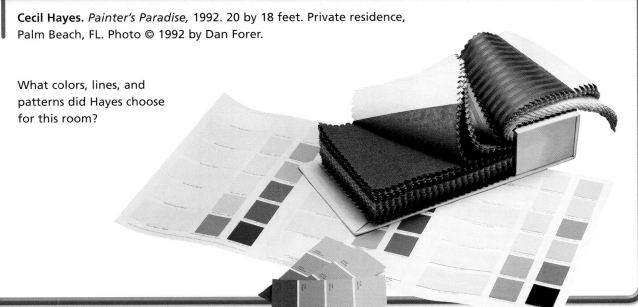

Design a Logo

A logo is a symbol for a group, such as a company or a club. Follow the steps to design a logo.

1 Think of symbols that stand for your school or for groups or clubs.

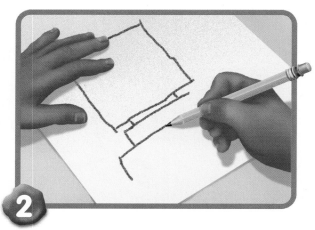

2 Design a logo for a group or club you are interested in.

3 Use lines and shapes to create an image. You may also use letters.

4 Color your logo with colored pencils or markers.

Alifonso, Age 9. *Art Club.* Marker on paper.

Danielle, Age 8. *Tiger Club.* Marker on paper.

What messages do these logos made by students send about their groups or clubs?

Share Your Art

1. Point to the images you used in your logo.

2. Ask your classmates to describe your logo's message. Was it the message you intended?

Think About Art

Read the art words. Then point to a picture that matches a word. A picture can match more than one word.

industrial design   weft   fibers
warp   weave   rhythm

Write About Art

Find an example of an industrial design around you. Write a paragraph about whether you think it is safe, attractive, and useful.

Talk About Art

- Look at the artworks you created for this unit.
- Choose the most challenging artwork.
- Tell a friend how you made the artwork and why it was challenging.
- Describe the medium or media you used.

Frank Romero.
Collective Mural,
1995. Acrylic and oil
on wood, each 23½
by 23½ inches.
Private collection.
© Frank Romero.
Photo by Doug
Parker Studios.

Put It All Together

1. What objects does this artwork show?

2. Are the images by the same artist? Explain.

3. Why do you think the artist created this artwork? What makes you think so?

4. What other objects might the artist have shown?

Line

straight

curved

zigzag

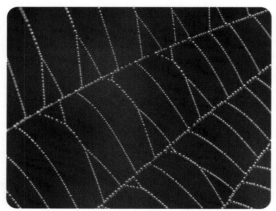

thin

thick

broken

Color

cool

warm

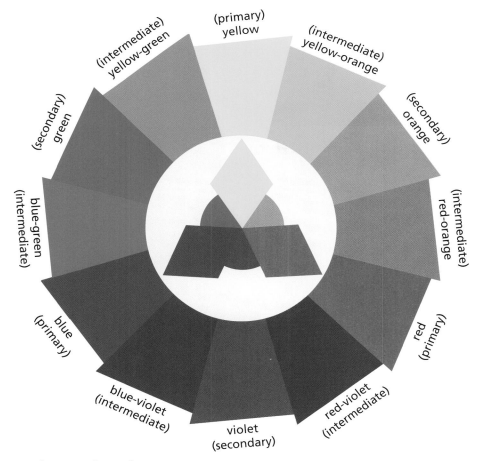

(primary)
yellow

(intermediate)
yellow-orange

(secondary)
orange

(intermediate)
red-orange

red
(primary)

red-violet
(intermediate)

violet
(secondary)

blue-violet
(intermediate)

blue
(primary)

blue-green
(intermediate)

(secondary)
green

(intermediate)
yellow-green

color wheel

Value

Shape

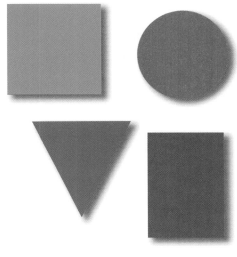

geometric shapes | organic shapes

Elements of Art

Texture

bumpy

soft

shiny

prickly

sticky

fluffy

Form

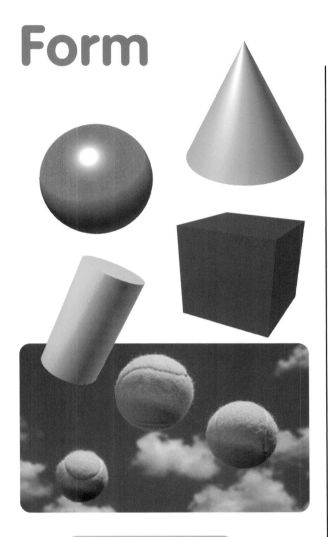

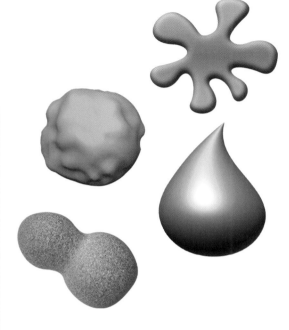

geometric forms

organic forms

Space

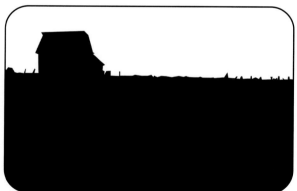

positive space

negative space

Principles of Design

Unity

Principles of Design

Variety

Emphasis

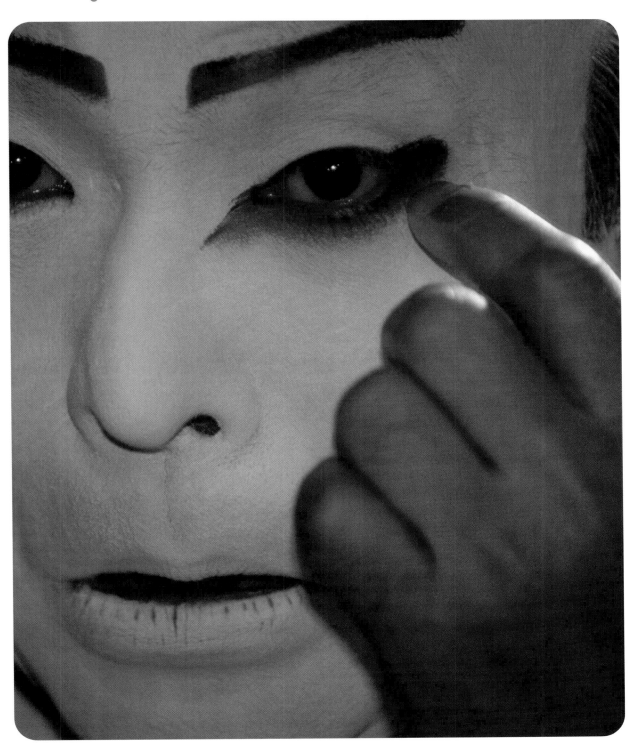

Balance

Proportion

Pattern

Rhythm

Think Safety

Read these safety rules. Be sure to follow these rules when you create artworks.

1. Keep art materials away from your face, especially your mouth and eyes.

2. Be careful when you work with scissors. If you use a sharp object, point it away from your body.

3. Read the labels on art materials. Look for the word *nontoxic*. This label tells you the materials are safe to use.

4. Do not breathe chalk dust or art sprays.

5. If you have a problem with any art materials, ask your teacher for help.

6. If an art material makes you feel sick, tell your teacher right away.

7. If you spill water or paint on the floor, be sure to clean it up quickly. A wet floor is unsafe to walk on.

8. Clean up after you finish an artwork. First, wash your hands with soap and water. Then, wash the tools you want to save, such as paintbrushes. Return art materials to their proper places.

Can you think of more ways to be safe?

List of Artists

Unknown Artists

Artists

List of Artists

Glossary

A

abstract [ab strakt´] A style of art in which the subject of an artwork has been simplified or rearranged. Abstract art emphasizes moods and impressions and is characterized by the use of bold colors, lines, and flat shapes.

Abstract Expressionist [ab strakt´ ik spre´ shə nist] An artist who uses an abstract style of art to show the main feeling or action of the subject. Artists developed this style in the United States shortly after World War II.

actual line A line that is real. It is a line you can actually see.

additive method [a´ də tiv me´ thəd] A method of creating a sculpture by combining, attaching, or adding separate parts to create a whole. Assemblages and welded metal sculptures are examples of artwork created through this method.

arch A curved structure that spans an opening.

architecture [är´ kə tek chər] The art and science of designing buildings and other large-scale, functional structures.

armature [är´ mə chür] In sculpture, a framework used to support material, such as clay or papier-mâché, that is being formed.

assemblage [ə sem´ blij] A type of three-dimensional art created by combining and connecting a variety of objects to create a pleasing whole.

asymmetrical [ā sə me´ tri kəl] **balance** A type of balance in which two sides of an artwork are not alike but carry equal or nearly equal visual weight. It is also known as *informal balance*.

asymmetry [ā si´ mə trē] A type of balance that lacks symmetry.

B

background The part of an artwork that appears to be farthest from the viewer, often in the distance of a scene.

balance The arrangement of the parts of an artwork to give an overall sense of equality in visual weight. Balance can be symmetrical, asymmetrical, or radial. Balance is a principle of design.

basket A hollow vessel created by weaving together stiff fibers such as twigs or reeds.

batik [bə tēk´] A method of decorating fabric that involves the use of wax and dye. A design is drawn on the fabric with melted wax. The fabric is then dipped in dye, and the parts that are covered in wax do not soak up the dye. The wax is then removed, revealing the design against the dye-colored background.

brayer [brā´ ər] In printing, a rubber roller used to spread ink over a surface.

carving The creation of a three-dimensional artwork by cutting away extra parts of a hard material, such as wood or stone. Also, a carved artwork.

center of interest The part of an artwork the viewer notices first. It is the most important part of an artwork.

close-up view A point of view in which objects in an artwork appear to be very near the viewer.

color The visual quality of objects, as they reflect hues on the color wheel, caused by the amount of light reflected by them. Color is an element of art.

color families Groups of related colors. For example, warm colors and cool colors are color families.

composition [käm pə zi´ shən] The arrangement of the various parts of an artwork into a pleasing whole. Composition also refers to a work of art.

computer technology Electronic and digital products related to computers.

computer-aided animation Animation, or moving pictures, created with the help of a computer.

contrast To show a large difference between two elements of art.

cool colors Related colors that range from green through blue and violet. Cool colors bring to mind cool objects, places, and feelings.

credit line The information in small type that accompanies a photograph of an artwork. It usually includes the artist's name, title of the artwork, date the artwork was completed, medium used, dimensions, and current owner or location of the artwork.

depth The distance between the front of something to the back.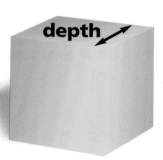

detail A small part of an artwork that has been pulled out and usually enlarged for close inspection. A detail is also a tiny or an especially interesting part of an artwork.

diagonal [dī ag´ nəl] **line** A line that slants in one direction. It is neither vertical nor horizontal.

digital camera A camera that takes pictures without using film.

dye [dī´] A substance used to give color to materials.

elements of art The basic parts of an artwork, including line, color, value, shape, texture, form, and space.

emboss [im bäs´] To create a raised design on a surface by pressing into the back of the material.

emphasis [em´ fə səs] The visual accent, stress, or sense of importance created in an artwork by the color, size, shape, or placement of an object or area. Emphasis is a principle of design.

exhibition [ek sə bi´ shən] A public showing of a collection of artworks.

express [ik spres´] To make one's thoughts or feelings known to others, often through words, gestures, or visual artworks.

expression [ik spre´ shən] The emotional display of an artist through an artwork, or a facial look that conveys a feeling.

Expressionistic [ik spre shə nis´ tik] A style of art in which the artist boldly expresses personal experiences and emotions about a subject using simple designs and brillant colors. Expressionism began in Germany during the early 1900s. It became popular in the United States during the 1940s and 1950s.

fabric A cloth made by knitting or weaving together fibers or threads.

fiber A natural or synthetic thread-like material often used for weaving or sewing. Fibers make up yarn, string, fabric, and other similar materials.

folk art Artwork that often reflects traditions of a particular culture, especially images made by artists who do not have formal training. Instead, they are usually self-taught or learn from their friends and relatives.

foreground The part of an artwork that appears to be nearest the viewer.

form A three-dimensional object, such as a cube or a sphere, that is shown in three-dimensional artworks. Form is defined by height, depth, and width. Form is an element of art.

found objects Any existing item that an artist finds and uses in an artwork. Found objects can be manufactured items, such as automobile parts, or natural objects, such as shells and feathers.

found-object sculpture [skəlp´ chər] A three-dimensional artwork that is composed of manufactured or natural objects found by the artist.

front view In an artwork, a view of the front side of an object or person.

full view A complete view of a person or object.

G

geometric [jē ə me´ trik] **shape**
A shape that is mathematically defined or regular in appearance, such as a triangle, circle, square, or rectangle.

German Expressionist
[ik spre´ shə nist] Any one of a group of artists, known as *The Blue Rider,* who worked in Germany in the early 1900s. The German Expressionists used bright, bold colors and expressed feelings in their artworks.

Gabriele Münter. *Jaulensky and Werefkin,* 1908–1909.

graphic design [gra´ fik di zīn´]
The design and often the production of commercial artworks, such as signs, posters, advertisements, book jackets, and computer software.

H

height The measurement of an object from the base to the top.

height

horizontal [hȯr ə zän´ təl] **line**
The direction of a line running straight across, parallel to the horizon.

hue [hyü´] Another word for color.

I

illustration [i les trā´ shən] A picture, often a drawing or painting, created mostly to be shown in books, magazines, or other printed works. An illustration helps explain something, or it tells a story.

Conrad Dielitz. *The Sleeping Beauty,* 1879.

implied line A line that is not shown but is implied, or suggested, by the placement of other lines, shapes, and colors.

industrial design
[in dəs´ trē əl di zīn´] The design of objects, such as automobiles, appliances, and telephones, that are manufactured and sold by industry.

intermediate [in tər mē´ dē ət] **color** A color created when a primary color (yellow, red, or blue) is mixed with a secondary color (orange, violet, or green). Some examples are red-violet and blue-green.

landscape architecture
[är´ kə tek chər] The planning and design of outdoor areas.

line The thin path of a point usually created by a pen, pencil, or paintbrush. Lines can be actual or implied. A line can be thick or thin and can be curved, straight, zigzag, dotted, wavy, spiral, or broken. Line is an element of art.

line direction The angle of a line. The direction of a line may be horizontal, vertical, or diagonal.

loom [lüm´] A frame-like tool used to hold fibers for weaving fabric.

media [mē´ dē ə] The materials used to create artworks, such as charcoal, pastels, oil paints, or clay. Media also refers to the techniques used to make an artwork, such as painting, sculpting, or drawing. The singular of *media* is *medium*.

middle ground The part of an artwork that appears to lie between the foreground and the background.

mood The overall feeling created in an artwork.

negative space The empty space that surrounds a form or shape in an artwork.

neutrals [nü´ trəls] A term used for black, white, and tints and shades of gray. Some artists also consider browns to be neutral.

nonobjective [nän əb jek´ tiv] **style** A term used to describe artworks that have no recognizable subject matter. This style does not represent real objects.

object Something in an artwork that usually can be named by the viewer.

organic shape Shapes and forms that are irregular, particularly those resembling objects in nature, such as the shape of a leaf or the form of an animal.

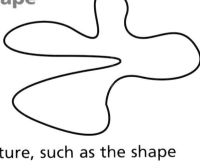

overlap To partly or completely cover one shape or form with another.

papier-mâché [pā pər mə shā´] A material made from paper pulp that can be molded when wet and painted when dry. It is also the technique for making sculptures from this material.

pattern Repetition of colors, lines, shapes, or forms in an artwork. Pattern is a principle of design. Also, a pattern is a plan or model to be followed when making something.

photograph [fo´ tə graf] An image recorded by a camera on film. The image can be printed on photosensitive paper, or if the camera is digital, the image can be shown on a computer screen.

photographer [fə tä´ grə fər] A person who takes photographs.

photomontage [fō tō män täzh´] An artwork made by combining parts of different photographs.

portrait
[pōr´ trət] An artwork that features a person, an animal, or a group of people, often placing emphasis on the face.

Christian Pierre. *Troy*, 1962.

positive space Shapes, forms, or lines that stand out from the background or negative space in an artwork.

primary color One of the three colors (yellow, red, and blue) from which other colors are made.

principles of design Guidelines artist use to arrange elements of art. The principles of design are unity, variety, emphasis, balance, proportion, pattern, and rhythm.

print An artwork created by coating a surface, such as a carved wood block, with wet color and then pressing paper onto it. The paper is "pulled" as a print.

printing block A surface, such as wood or linoleum, into which an artist carves a design. Ink or paint is spread across the surface and paper is pressed onto it to make a print, an impression of the design.

proportion [prə pōr´ shən] The size relationship of one part of an artwork to another part or the whole. For example, the size relationship of the nose to the face shows proportion. Proportion is a principle of design.

Q

quilt [kwilt´] A padded bedcover made from two layers of cloth that are sewn together with stuffing in between. Usually, one layer is made from scraps of fabric that have been arranged and  stitched together in a colorful design. Also, the term is used to mean creating a quilt.

R

radial [rā´ dē əl] **balance** A type of balance in which lines or shapes spread out from a center point.

realistic [rē ə lis´ tik] A style of art that describes artworks showing objects and scenes as they actually look to most viewers.

related colors Colors, such as yellow, yellow-orange, and orange, that are next to each other on the color wheel. They are also called *analogous colors*.

relief [ri lēf´] **print** An artwork made by rolling ink onto a carved surface showing a raised design and then pressing paper onto it.

relief sculpture [ri lēf´ skəlp´ chər] A kind of sculpture that stands out from a flat background.

resist [ri zist´] A material, such as wax, used to protect parts of a surface from paint or dye.

rhythm [ri´ thəm] A sense of visual movement or motion caused by the repetition of one or more elements of art, such as color, line, shape, or form, in an artwork. Rhythm is a principle of design.

S

sculpture [skəlp´ chər] An artwork made by modeling, carving, or joining materials into a three-dimensional whole. Clay, wood, stone, and metal are some common materials used for sculpture. Sculpture is also the process of making such an artwork.

secondary color A color created by mixing two primary colors. The secondary colors are orange (made from yellow and red), violet (made from red and blue), and green (made from blue and yellow).

self-portrait [self´ pōr´ trət] An artwork showing a likeness of the artist who created it.

shade A darker value created by adding black to a color or by adding black to white.

shape A two-dimensional flat area made by lines that enclose it. A shape can be geometric, such as a circle or square, or organic, having an irregular outline. Shape is an element of art.

size proportion See *proportion*.

space An open or empty surface or area. Shapes and forms show empty space surrounding them (negative space) and the space they occupy (positive space). Space is an element of art.

still life An artwork showing an arrangement of objects that do not move on their own.

Erik Slutsky. *Memories of Aix, 2000.*

story quilt [kwilt´] A quilt showing pictures and words that tell a story.

studio [stü´ dē ō] A room or workshop where an artist works.

style An artist's own special way of creating art through the use of specific media, methods, materials, or subjects. Artistic style can also represent certain techniques of a group of artists in a specific culture or time.

subtractive method [səb trak´ tiv me´ thəd] A method of creating a sculpture by carving, cutting, or otherwise removing excess material from a block of wood, stone, clay, or other substance.

subtractive process [səb trak´ tiv prō´ səs] See *subtractive method*.

symbol [sim´ bəl] A letter, color, sign, or picture used to represent a word, message, or idea. For example, a red heart is often used as a symbol for love.

246

symmetrical [sə me´ tri kəl] **balance** A type of balance in which both sides of a center line are the same or about the same. A cat's face, for example, is symmetrically balanced along a vertical line through the middle of the nose. Symmetrical balance is also known as *formal balance*.

symmetry [si´ mə trē] Balance created by making both sides of an artwork the same or about the same.

---

tactile texture [tak´ təl teks´ chər] Texture that can be understood by the sense of touch. It is also called *actual texture*. Tactile textures, which artists show in their compositions, include rough, smooth, silky, pebbly, soft, hard, bumpy, and scratchy. See *texture*.

texture [teks´ chər] The way a surface feels (actual or tactile texture) or looks (visual texture). Words such as shiny, dull, rough, and smooth are used to describe texture. Texture is an element of art.

three-dimensional Having height, width, and depth or thickness. Something that is three-dimensional is not a flat shape. It is a form.

three-quarter view A view of a subject that is halfway between the angles of a profile and a frontal view.

tint A light value of a color created by mixing the color with white.

two-dimensional Having height and width but not depth. Something that is two-dimensional is flat.

---

unity [yü´ nə tē] A quality that occurs when all parts of an artwork combine to create a sense of wholeness and completion. Unity is a principle of design.

---

value [val´ yü] The lightness or darkness of a color. Tints have a light value. Shades have a dark value. For example, pink is a light value of red, while navy is a dark value of blue. Value is an element of art.

variety [və rī´ ə tē] The combination of elements of art, such as line, shape, or color that adds interest to an artwork. Variety is a principle of design.

vertical [vər´ ti kəl] A direction running straight up and down.

visual texture [vi´ zhə wəl teks´ chər] The way a surface appears through the sense of vision. For example, the surface of a sculpture may be shiny or dull. See *texture*.

warm colors The family of related colors that range from yellow through orange and red. Warm colors usually remind people of warm objects, places, and feelings.

warp [wȯrp´] In weaving, fibers stretched vertically, top to bottom, on a loom and through which the weft is woven.

weave [wēv´] To make cloth-like artworks by interlacing, or weaving, warp and weft threads, or other fiber, often on a loom.

weft In weaving, fibers woven over and under, from side to side, through the warp on a loom.

width The measurement of an object across from one side to the other.

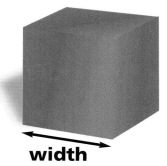

width

Index

Index

Acknowledgments

ILLUSTRATIONS

20, 21, 24, 25, 28, 29, 34, 35, 38, 39, 42, 43, 54, 55, 58, 59, 62, 63, 68, 69, 72, 73, 76, 77, 88, 89, 92, 93, 96, 97, 102, 103, 106, 107, 110, 111, 122, 123, 126, 127, 130, 131, 136, 137, 140, 141, 144, 145, 156, 157, 160, 161, 164, 165, 170, 171, 174, 175, 178, 179, 190, 191, 194, 195, 198, 199, 204, 205, 208, 209, 212, 213 Meryl Treatner

46, 80, 114, 148, 182, 216 Ron Berg

PHOTOGRAPHS

Every effort has been made to secure permission and provide appropriate credit for photographic material. The publisher deeply regrets any omission and pledges to correct errors called to its attention in subsequent editions.

Unless otherwise acknowledged, all photographs are the property of Scott Foresman, a division of Pearson Education.

Photo locators denoted as follows: Top (t), Center (c), Bottom (b), Left (l), Right (r), Background (Bkgd)

Front Matter

Page iv(bl), © 1998 Faith Ringgold; 2(bl), The Menil Collection, Houston; 3(br), Bequest of Edward L. Whittmore, 1930.191, © The Cleveland Museum of Art; 7(b), © Francisco Cruz/SuperStock; 7, © Fenimore Art Museum, Cooperstown, NY/Art Resource, New York; 10, © Art Resource, NY; 14, © 2004 The Georgia O'Keeffe Foundation/Artists Rights Society (ARS), New York.

Units 1–6

Page 16, © 1998 Faith Ringgold; 17, Portrait of Faith Ringgold with detail of "The Purple Quilt." Photograph, © C'Love, 1986; 18, © Francis G. Mayer/Corbis; 23, Palmer C. Hayden Collection. Gift of Miriam A. Hayden. The Museum of African American Art, Los Angeles; 27(tr), © 1980 Carmen Lomas Garza. Collection of Richard L. Bains and Amalia Mesa-Bains, San Francisco, CA; 27, Getty Images; 30, © Faith Ringgold, 1988. Courtesy of the artist; 31, © Christie's Images/Corbis; 32, © 2004 The Georgia O'Keeffe Foundation/Artists Rights Society (ARS), New York; 33, Getty Images; 33, © Jose Luis Pelaez, Inc./Corbis; 36, National Portrait Gallery, Smithsonian Institution/Art Resource, NY; 37, © Goodshoot/SuperStock; 44(bl), Courtesy of Winnie Lambrecht, RI State Council on the Arts; 44(br), © Jacqui Hurst/Corbis; 45, Museum of International Folk Art, Santa Fe, NM; 48, © Ray Juno/Corbis; 48, © Jacqui Hurst/Corbis; 48, © Sampson Williams/SuperStock; 49, Giraudon/Bridgeman Art Library. © 2004 Artists Rights Society (ARS), New York/ADAGP, Paris; 50, M. C. Escher's *Rind* © 2003/Cordon Art B.V.-Baarn-Holland. All rights reserved; 51, M. C. Escher. *Self-Portrait*, 1929. Lithograph, 10 3/8 by 8 inches. © 2003 Cordon Art B.V., Baarn, Holland. All rights reserved; 56, Collection of The McNay Art Museum, Gift of the Estate of Tom Slick. © 2004 The Georgia O'Keeffe Foundation/Artists Rights Society (ARS), New York; 57, © Dale Jorgensen/SuperStock; 57, © Jim Richardson/Corbis; 60, © 2004 Artists Rights Society (ARS), New York/VG Bild Kunst, Bonn; 64, © 2003 Cordon Art B.V., Baarn, Holland. All rights reserved; 65, Photo by Earlie Hudnall, Hudnall's Positive Images; 66, © Réunion des Musées Nationaux/Art Resource, NY; 70, The Art Institute of Chicago. Robert A. Waller Fund, 1910.2; 71, Erich Lessing/Art Resource NY; 75, © Smithsonian American Art Museum, Washington, D.C./Art Resource, NY; 78(br), © Rachel Cobb; 78(b), © Myrleen F. Cate/PhotoEdit; 79, © Rachel Cobb; 82, © SuperStock; 82, © SuperStock; 83, © Janet Fish/ Licensed by VAGA, New York, NY. Photo by Aindman/Fremont, Abudefduf, Inc., New York; 84, © Tate Gallery, London/Art Resource, NY. © Henry Moore Foundation; 85, © David Lees/Corbis; 86, © Larry Lee/Corbis; 86, © Roger Ressmeyer/Corbis; 86, © Corbis; 90, © L. Willinger/SuperStock; 91(tl), Photo © Brett Patterson/Corbis. © Claes Oldenburg and Coosje van Bruggen; 95, Musée du quai Branly, Paris. Ancient Collection Guy Joussemet. Photo by Hughes Dubois, © Musée du Quai Branly; 91, © Getty Images; 94, The Menil Collection, Houston; 98, © Boltin Picture Library, Croton-

Acknowledgments

on-Hudson, New York. © Henry Moore Foundation; 101, © Fenimore Art Museum, Cooperstown, NY/Art Resource, NY; 104, Metropolitan Museum of Art, Rogers Fund, 1947 (47.100.1). Photograph © 1996 The Metropolitan Museum of Art; 108, © 2004 Estate of Alexander Calder/Artists Rights Society (ARS), New York; 109, © Burnstien Collection/Corbis. © 2004 Estate of Louise Nevelson/ Artists Rights Society (ARS), New York; 112, Nam June Paik in his installation *Fish Flies on Sky*, 1976. Photograph by Peter Moore, © 1998 Estate of Peter Moore/Licensed by VAGA, New York, NY; 113, Carl Solway Gallery, Inc.; 116, Jan Butchofsky-Houser/Corbis; 116, Jonathan Blair/Corbis; 118, Collection of the Montreal Museum of Fine Arts, Purchase, John W. Tempest Fund. Photograph by Christine Guest, MBAM/MMFA; 119, Reproduced and published by Bunshichi Kobayashi. Woodcut print from original drawing, 23 2/3 by 10 inches. Sumida City Tokyo, Peter Morse Collection; 120, The Metropolitan Museum of Art. H. O. Havemeyer Collection. Bequest of Mrs. H. O. Havemeyer, 1929. 29.100.113. Photograph © 1996 The Metropolitan Museum of Art; 121, © Giraudon/Art Resource, New York; 124, © SuperStock; 125, © Smithsonian American Art Museum, Washington, D.C./Art Resource, NY; 128 © Fiduciario en el Fideicomiso relativo a los Museos Diego Rivera y Frida Kahlo. Reproduction authorized by the Bank of Mexico, Mexico City; 129, © National Gallery, Prague/Art Resource, New York; 132, © Fine Arts Museums of San Francisco, Acenbach Foundation for Graphic Arts, Gift of Patricia Brown McNamara, Jane Brown Dunaway, and Helen Brown Jarman, in memory of Mary Wattis Brown, 64.47.111; 133, © Réunion des Musées Nationaux/Art Resource, NY; 134, © Private Collection/Bridgeman Art Library; 135, © Erich Lessing/Art Resource, NY; 138, © Roy Rainford/Robert Harding Picture Library; 139(tl), © Dallas and John Heaton/Corbis; 139, © Richard Klune/Corbis; 142, Courtesy of The Harvard Fogg Museum, Harvard University Art Museums. Gift of the family and friends of Howard Mueliner, Class of 1962, in his memory;143 © The Cleveland Museum of Art, 2003. Bequest of Edward L. Whittemore 1930.191; 146(b), Rodney Freeman; 147(t), Rodney Freeman; 147(br), Getty Images; 150, © Bob Krist/Corbis; 150, © Ludovic Maisant/Corbis; 153(bc), © Norman Parkinson Limited/ Fiona Cowan/Corbis; 154, © 1991/Faith Ringgold; 158, Städtische Galerie im Lenbachhaus, Munich; 159, Photograph by David Heald © 2003 The Solomon R. Guggenheim Foundation/Peggy Guggenheim Collection, Venice (Solomon R. Guggenheim Foundation, NY); 162, Library of Congress; 169, Gift of Mr. and Mrs. Armand J. Castellani, 1981, Albright-Knox Art Gallery, Buffalo, New York; 172, © Karen Guzak. Courtesy of the artist; 176, © Reagan Bradshaw; 180, © Claudia Calle; 181, © Daniel Portnoy; 184, © Jacqui Hurst/Corbis; 184, © SuperStock; 184, © Ping Amranand/SuperStock; 187, Art © Nancy Graves Foundation, Photograph by Robin Holland/ Licensed by VAGA, New York, NY; 192, National Museum of Natural History. © 2003 Smithsonian Institution; 193, John Bigelow Taylor/Art Resource, NY; 196, © Victoria & Albert Museum, London/ Art Resource, NY; 197, Courtesy of Ceci Phillips, Austin, Texas; 201, © Smithsonian American Art Museum, Washington, D.C./Art Resource, NY; 206, Richard Wilde and Silas H. Rhodes, Art Directors; William J. Kobasz, Designer; Dee Ito, Copywriter. Courtesy of the School of Visual Arts, New York; 207, © 20th Century Fox/The Kobal Collection; 214, © Cecil Hayes; 214(br), © Corbis; 215(t), © Dan Forer; 218, © Corbis; 218(tr), © Getty Images; 218(cr), © The Lowe Art Museum, The University of Miami/SuperStock.

Back Matter

Page 220, © Getty Images; 220, © Getty Images; 220, © Corbis; 220, © Getty Images; 221, © Getty Images; 221, digitalvisiononline.com; 222, © Darrell Gulin/Corbis; 222, © Eric Crichton/Corbis; 223, © Paul Chauncey/Corbis; 223, Corbis; 223, © Pat Doyle/Corbis; 224, © Robert Yin/Corbis; 224, ©David Frazier/Corbis; 224, © Peter Dazeley/Corbis; 224, © Richard Hamilton Smith/Corbis; 224, © Charles Gold/Corbis; 224, © Lance Nelson/Corbis; 225, © The Purcell Team/Corbis; 225, © Lindsey P. Martin/Corbis; 225, © Nik Wheeler/Corbis; 227, © Randy Faris/Corbis; 228, © Bob Krist/Corbis; 229, © Charles & Josette Lenars/Corbis; 230, © Mark Gibson/Corbis; 231, © Tom Bean/Corbis; 232, © Corbis; 233, © Getty Images; 238, © Richard Cummins/SuperStock; 239, © Corbis; 241, © Jose Luis Pelaez, Inc./Corbis; 242(cl), Städtische Galerie Im Lenbachhaus, Munich; 242(cr), A. K. G. Berlin/ SuperStock; 244, © Christian Pierre/SuperStock; 245, © Roman Soumar/Corbis; 245, © Isy Ochoa/ SuperStock; 246, © Erik Slutsky/SuperStock; 246, © Annie Griffiths Belt/Corbis; 247, © Francisco Cruz/SuperStock; 248, © Corbis.